LAKE FOREST LIBRARY
3 1243 00246 2421

D1360600

Theodore Roosevelt

Series Consultant:
Don M. Coerver, professor of history
Texas Christian University, Fort Worth, Texas

Michael A. Schuman

Enslow Publishers, Inc.

44 Fadem Road
Box 699
Springfield, NJ 07081
USA

PO Box 38
Aldershot
Hants GU12 6BP
UK

To my friend Howard Manas, who always insures that there will be at least one correct vote in New Jersey.

Library of Congress Cataloging-in-Publication Data

Schuman, Michael.
Theodore Roosevelt / Michael A. Schuman.
p. cm. — (United States presidents)
Includes bibliographical references and index.
Summary: Explores the life of the twenty-sixth president, from his childhood in New York, through his military career, to his years in the White House.
ISBN 0-89490-836-7
1. Roosevelt, Theodore, 1858–1919—Juvenile literature. 2. Presidents—United States—Biography—Juvenile literature. 3. United States—Politics and government—1901–1909—Juvenile literature. [1. Roosevelt, Theodore, 1858–1919. 2. Presidents.]
I. Title. II. Series.
E757.S38 1997
973.91'1'092—dc21
[B]
97-7272
CIP
AC

Printed in the United States of America

10 9 8 7 6 5 4 3 2 1

Illustration Credits: Portsmouth Atheneum, p. 9; National Park Service, U.S. Department of the Interior, p. 12; Sagamore Hill National Historic Site, pp. 15, 17, 21, 26, 28, 37, 41, 47, 58, 63, 72, 93, 95, 102; Library of Congress, pp. 70, 78; College Football Hall of Fame, p. 76; FDR Library, p. 110.

Source Document Credits: *Theodore Roosevelt's Letters to His Children* (Scribner's, 1919), pp. 67, 69; National Archives, pp. 45, 49, 65, 88, 89; In William A. DeGregorio, *The Complete Book of U.S. Presidents* (New York: Dembner Books, 1984), pp. 56, 74, 107; Upton Sinclair, *The Jungle* (New York: The New American Library, 1964), p. 80; In Joseph Nathan Kane, *Facts About the Presidents: A Compilation of Biographical and Historical Information,* 6th ed. (New York: The H.W. Wilson Company, 1993), p. 97.

Cover Illustration: Copyrighted by the White House Historical Association.

Contents

Acknowledgments

Many thanks to: the staffs at the library at Keene State College and the Keene Public Library, to John Gable of the Theodore Roosevelt Association, to Kathleen Young-Sheedy and Amy Verone at Sagamore Hill, to Mark Comito at the Theodore Roosevelt Inaugural National Historic Site and to Bernie Kish and Kent Stephens at the College Football Hall of Fame. And thanks so much to my wife Patti, who sometimes thought I was married to this book instead of her.

1

THE PEACEFUL WARRIOR

Bullets and torpedoes were being fired through the air and waters of the Far East in 1904. People were dying in droves. Russia and Japan were at war. The two countries were fighting for control of land in the Pacific.

Like all wars, the results of the Russo-Japanese War were tragic. After sixteen months, over eighty thousand Japanese soldiers had died of either battle wounds or disease.[1]

The Russians were having it worse. The war began with a surprise attack by Japan in February 1904. Much of Russia's Pacific naval fleet was destroyed.

Then the Russians lost one battle after another. During a long battle over a city in China called Mukden

(today Shenyang), two hundred thousand Russians were killed or injured.[2]

One Russian seaman wrote of the violence,

> Now the injured were coming or being brought in thick and fast: men with . . . bones broken, skulls fractured. Some were so badly burned as to be unrecognizable; they shivered pitifully, moaning: "I'm so cold, so bitterly cold."[3]

On the other side of the world, United States President Theodore Roosevelt was well aware of the horrors of war. He had served in battle in the Spanish-American War seven years earlier. In the Russo-Japanese War, the United States was neutral. The United States hoped that neither Japan nor Russia would gain too much control in the region. That could hurt the United States' standing in the Far East.

Japan was the stronger of the two warring nations. However, by the spring of 1905, Japan was weary. Its leaders did not want to suggest on their own that the war be ended. Russia might interpret that as a sign of weakness. So they secretly asked Roosevelt to invite Russia to work out a peace treaty with them. Roosevelt agreed to the offer, but his job would be a difficult one.

The head of Russia was Czar Nicholas II. (A czar was similar to an emperor.) Nicholas would not allow Russian diplomats to meet with Japan. Russia's view was that the war was based partly on race. They felt that the white race was fighting an inferior Asian race. A Russian diplomat named Count Cassini added "that Russia was too great to admit defeat."[4]

Roosevelt was frustrated. He exclaimed, "Oh Lord! I have been going nearly mad in the effort to get Russia and Japan together."[5]

Czar Nicholas's cousin was the leader of Germany. His name was Kaiser Wilhelm II. (The kaiser was the German equal to the Russian czar.) Roosevelt came up with the idea of approaching Nicholas through his cousin. Wilhelm believed that any more fighting would cause unrest in Russia which might spill over into his own country. In June, Wilhelm sent a letter to Nicholas supporting peace talks. After receiving the letter from his cousin, Nicholas accepted.

Now the true hard work began. It took weeks before a location for the meeting was chosen. Japan wanted to meet in China, while Russia favored Europe. It was finally decided to meet in a neutral land, the United States.

Washington, D.C., was ruled out. It was hot and muggy in the summer and air conditioning did not exist then. A New England coastal setting was thought to be a good idea. The quiet resort town of Portsmouth, New Hampshire, was selected.

Czar Nicholas sent representatives to meet with Roosevelt. Japan's leader, Emperor Mutsu Hito Meiji, did the same. The statesmen got together for the first time on the presidential yacht on August 5, 1905. This was not in Portsmouth, but off the coast of Oyster Bay, New York. Oyster Bay was Roosevelt's home when he was not at the White House.

Roosevelt had to be careful not to appear to favor either country, even by accident. If one country's diplomat entered a formal room before the other, Roosevelt could be seen as playing favorites. The President solved that problem by entering the yacht's dining room with a Japanese diplomat on one side and a Russian on the other.

The Japanese and Russian diplomats left for Portsmouth. Roosevelt stayed in Oyster Bay. The two countries first met on August 9 and agreed on some terms right away. However, there were two sticking points.

Japan wanted money in exchange for damages caused by Russia during the war. This type of payment is called an indemnity. Japan also wanted possession of an island called Sakhalin. It is located off the eastern coast of Russia and is north of Japan. The Russians were occupying it.

Russia refused to give in. The two sides were deadlocked. On August 29, the Russian delegates received orders to return home. Russia was ready to go back to war.

Although Roosevelt stayed away from Portsmouth, he worked behind the scenes. He communicated with the Russian and Japanese diplomats by way of telegraph and telephone from his home in Oyster Bay. Roosevelt tried to convince Japan to drop the demand for money. Then he told the Russians that continuing the war would only cause more death and hardship.

Theodore Roosevelt (center) is shown here with the Russian and Japanese diplomats, on the Mayflower *at Oyster Bay during the peace talks that ended the Russo-Japanese War.*

Finally, Japan made one more offer. They would drop the request for money if Russia left Sakhalin. The Russians offered a compromise of dividing the island in two. Japan accepted. A peace treaty was drawn up. Roosevelt went to Portsmouth to sign it on September 5. It was called the Treaty of Portsmouth. The Russo-Japanese War was over. Roosevelt was praised by leaders across the globe. However, his greatest honor was winning the highest tribute to any statesman—the Nobel Peace Prize. He was President Theodore Roosevelt—peacemaker!

2

A SICKLY BOY

Theodore Roosevelt, Jr., was born on October 27, 1858 to one of the wealthiest families in New York City. His father, Theodore, Sr., was in the family's glass-importing business. The Roosevelts' ancestors had been in the United States for over two hundred years. The first Roosevelt came to America from Holland some time before 1648.[1]

Theodore, Jr.'s mother came from a well-to-do family in Georgia. Her name before marriage was Martha Bulloch, but everyone called her Mittie. The Bulloch family had been in America since 1729. Yet compared to the Roosevelts, the Bullochs were newcomers.

Theodore, Jr., was called Teedie as a boy. He grew up in a house located in a neighborhood near Gramercy Park in Manhattan. Some of the richest families in the

Theodore Roosevelt grew up in this brownstone house near Gramercy Park in Manhattan, New York.

city lived there. Today the area is filled with businesses. In 1858, though, it was quiet and the streets were lined with trees and private homes.

Most houses there were tall, narrow buildings attached to one another. They were made of sandstone and called brownstones because of their color. Teedie's first home was a typical one. The furniture was formal. A rough material called haircloth covered the dining room chairs. Roosevelt later recalled how the haircloth chairs "scratched the bare legs of the children when they sat on it."[2] He also remembered the library in his house as being "gloomy."[3]

Like many wealthy families in those days, the Roosevelts escaped the heat of the city in summer. It was a luxury most other New Yorkers could not afford. The Roosevelts spent their summers at cooler locations, such as upstate New York or the New Jersey shore. Teedie loved his days in the country. He picked apples, hunted frogs, and ran barefoot.

Though he enjoyed activity, Teedie was not healthy and robust. He remembered himself as "a sickly, delicate boy."[4] He suffered from a disease called asthma. People with asthma have sudden episodes in which they find it hard to breathe. They might also have tightness in their chest, along with wheezing and coughing.

In the most severe cases, people with asthma episodes say they feel as if they are drowning. They might wake up from a deep sleep gasping for air. They try their hardest to breathe but no air comes in. The fact that the worst attacks often come at night can be scary.

Remedies that were once used to treat asthma seem crazy today. When Teedie suffered an attack, his father would rush him into a carriage outdoors. Then they would drive at a fast clip through the city streets. It was believed that fast driving would force air into Teedie's feeble lungs.

Tobacco and caffeine in coffee were also thought to be cures. Teedie was forced to drink black coffee or smoke a cigar to counter an attack.

Teedie's health suffered in other ways, too. He often caught colds and ran high fevers. He also had a nervous stomach which caused painful stomachaches. Once he told his mother, "I have a toothache in my stomach."[5]

Teedie's family life was a solid one, with loving parents and a secure home. Something happened in April 1861 that could have changed all that. The Civil War broke out. The Northern states (the Union) were fighting the Southern states (the Confederacy). With one parent from Georgia and one from New York, the family might have easily been split apart.

In addition, Mittie had two brothers fighting for the Confederacy. Theodore, Sr., did not enlist in the Union Army. In his day, it was legal for a man to pay a substitute to serve in his place. The standard rate to hire one was about $1,000, which is equal today to about $10,000 to $15,000.[6] Only the rich could afford to hire substitutes. Theodore, Sr., was one of many who did.

Teedie was a sickly child who suffered from attacks of asthma.

Historians have given different reasons why Theodore, Sr., hired a substitute to fight for him. Most likely, it was out of respect for his wife.[7]

Though he did not fight, Theodore, Sr., did aid the Union war effort. He and two other businessmen helped persuade Congress to pass a law making it easier for soldiers to support their families. The law allowed soldiers to send a portion of their pay home at no extra charge.

Meanwhile, Mittie helped the Confederacy by sending packages of clothing and personal items for her friends and family in the South. She only did so when her husband was away. Since it was illegal to send goods to the Confederacy, she had to send her packages to the Bahamas. From there a friend would forward them to Mittie's family in Georgia.

Teedie was only two-and-a-half-years old when the war started. Although he was too young to understand what the fighting was about, he sided with his father. He played soldier in a children's Union military uniform. One night when saying his bedtime prayers, he asked God "to grind the southern troops to powder."[8]

Days after the war ended in 1865, President Abraham Lincoln was assassinated. His body was brought by train from Washington, D.C., to his home of Springfield, Illinois, to be buried. In cities along the way, funeral processions were held so the people of the United States could pay their respects. In these

Theodore Roosevelt's mother, Mittie, was from a wealthy Georgia family. During the Civil War, she tried to help the Confederacy by sending necessities to her family in the South.

processions, church bells rang mournfully and marchers dressed in black.

In New York City, the procession marched past the house of Teedie's grandfather. Teedie, his brother Elliott, and a small girl named Edith Kermit Carow watched from a second-story window. Edith, known as Edie, was a friend of Teedie's younger sister, Corinne, or Conie. Although Edie was four years old, she formed a special friendship with Teedie.

As they watched the funeral procession, Edie became frightened and started to cry. The scared girl bothered the boys, who made her go into another room.

After the war, life in the Roosevelt house returned to normal. One day in 1866, Teedie was walking at an outdoor market where he stumbled on something that fascinated him. A seal that had been killed in New York Harbor was laid out on a slab of wood.

He later wrote, "That seal filled me with every possible feeling of romance and adventure."[9]

Teedie went back for several days to look at the seal. He measured its size with a ruler and made notes about it. He was given the seal's skull, which he took home.

Teedie collected more animal specimens. Not all were dead. One time a live mouse climbed out of a block of cheese being passed around at the dinner table. Teedie called his collection the Roosevelt Museum of Natural History.

Like many wealthy families, the Roosevelts did not send their children to public schools. One reason was that people of their background did not mix with poorer persons. Another was that Theodore and Mittie were concerned that Teedie and their other children would pick up all sorts of illnesses. The Roosevelt children were taught by private tutors at home. The children's most frequent tutor was Mittie's sister, Teedie's Aunt Anna. She became a permanent resident in the home.

Thanks to his father, Teedie learned about the outside world in a special way. Theodore, Sr., was a generous man who spent much of his time and money helping others. With two other men, he founded the Children's Aid Society for homeless children in New York City.

Local police called these kids "street rats."[10] Theodore, Sr., saw them as children who had tough breaks and needed help. The purpose of the Children's Aid Society was to educate these children and give them decent homes.

Theodore also helped establish the Newsboys' Lodging House. It provided homeless boys a clean and safe place to sleep. Many of them sold or delivered newspapers for little money. When Theodore was asked to spend every other Sunday evening visiting the boys at the house, he refused. He promised to be there every Sunday.

Theodore, Sr., often took little Teedie with him on these visits. Small wonder why Roosevelt later wrote, "My father, Theodore Roosevelt, was the best man I ever knew."[11]

Theodore, Sr., also brought Teedie and his other children with him when the family traveled to Europe. This was a luxury few could afford. Teedie's first trip to Europe began in 1868 when he was ten. It lasted a year. His education was not ignored. Even in Europe, he had a private tutor.

Roosevelt later wrote that he "hated" that trip.[12] His private diary told a different story. In it he wrote that he had "fine fun" at historic sites.[13] He did get homesick, though. He wrote that he missed his playmate and friend, Edith Carow.[14]

Teedie also suffered from his usual asthma attacks and stomachaches. That made stretches of the trip unpleasant for both him and his parents.

Upon returning home, Theodore, Sr., had a heart-to-heart talk with Teedie. The father said to his son, "Theodore, you have the mind but you have not the body, and without the help of the body the mind cannot go as far as it should. You must make your body. It is hard drudgery to make one's body, but I know you will do it."[15]

Teedie agreed, and for several months his mother took him to a gymnasium to work out. Then his father had a private gym built on a porch in his home.

Teedie exercised regularly. As his father said, it was drudgery. There was no modern fitness equipment such as stationary bikes or stair machines. People exercised with free weights, punching bags, and parallel bars.

Theodore Roosevelt, Sr. (shown here), encouraged his son to condition his body as well as his mind.

Teedie repeated the boring routine, day after day after day.

It was also learned at the time that Teedie was nearsighted. He was fitted with eyeglasses (called spectacles then). Roosevelt later wrote, "I had no idea how beautiful the world was until I got those spectacles."[16]

Although his body grew stronger, he was still a meek-looking child with eyeglasses. Today someone like him might be called a nerd or a geek. When he was fourteen, he took a stagecoach trip alone to Maine. On board, he met two boys about his age. The boys picked on him for the entire trip. Teedie tried fighting back but was unable to defend himself.

He was humiliated.[17] Upon returning home Teedie asked his father for permission to take boxing lessons. His father agreed. Teedie began sparring with a former professional boxer named John Long. He practiced long and hard. In time he became a pretty skilled boxer.

When Teedie was fourteen, the family again sailed overseas. They spent time in Europe, Egypt, and Palestine (today the countries of Israel and Jordan). His favorite place was Egypt. He wrote home to Edith Carow, "I think I have enjoyed myself more this winter than I ever did before."[18]

When the Roosevelts returned, they moved into a bigger home in the city. They also began spending time at a family compound in the town of Oyster Bay on Long Island. At the time, Oyster Bay was mostly rural. Teedie, now fifteen, and Edie enjoyed long walks together through the woods. He even named his rowboat after her.

Theodore Roosevelt, Sr., wanted his son to attend Harvard University in Cambridge, Massachusetts. He hired a private tutor to prepare Teedie for entrance examinations.

Teedie continued exercising, and his health improved. The asthma attacks occurred less often. Teedie's mind was as sound as ever. He passed the Harvard entrance exams with little problem.

On September 27, 1876, Theodore Roosevelt, Jr., boarded the train that took him to Harvard University.

3

THE LIGHT FROM MY LIFE FOR EVER

Most of the students at Harvard were like Roosevelt. They were wealthy, white, and Protestant. Since women were not yet admitted to Harvard, all were male.

Yet Roosevelt was different in some ways. Most of his classmates were from Massachusetts. He also acted differently from many other students. It was fashionable for Harvard men to be laid back in the way they moved and talked. Roosevelt was lively and spirited. Other students at first found him to be an oddball.

He loved to talk. In one class he asked so many questions that a professor responded, "See here, Roosevelt, let me talk! I'm running this course."[1]

In time, his classmates began to see Roosevelt as an intelligent, friendly young man. He was still interested in natural history. In his apartment he kept snakes, lizards, and mounted birds. One friend named Robert Bacon was said to be so revolted by the animals in Roosevelt's room that he refused to go near it.

Roosevelt also continued boxing. He did not shine in the sport, but he was a tough competitor. In his junior year, Roosevelt made it to the championship round for lightweights in the Harvard Athletic Association's boxing competition. His opponent was a taller and stronger student named C. S. Hanks. Hanks won the match but Roosevelt won the respect of his classmates by lasting the entire fight.

Roosevelt earned very good grades in his courses. As he got older, his grades got even better. His body matured as well, and the asthma attacks and other illnesses decreased.

By now, Roosevelt was no longer known as Teedie. That was a little boy's name. To his friends, he was either Ted, Ted-o, or Teddy.

Tragedy struck Roosevelt in his sophomore year. His father died of stomach cancer in February 1878 at age forty-six. Roosevelt was depressed for a long time. Four months later, he wrote in his private diary, "Oh, Father, how bitterly I miss you and long for you."[2]

On the other hand, there were times of happiness. Roosevelt was a few days shy of his twentieth birthday when something special happened. He first set eyes on a willowy blonde named Alice Lee. She was a cousin and neighbor of one of Roosevelt's best college friends,

Theodore Roosevelt (top center, with the sideburns) is shown here with some of his Harvard classmates.

Dick Saltonstall. Alice lived with her family in the nearby town of Chestnut Hill. Roosevelt later said, "I loved her as soon as I saw her sweet, fair, young face."[3]

Alice was a popular, pretty girl. Because she was cheery and fun to be with, her friends called her "Sunshine." While Roosevelt saw her as a potential wife, seventeen-year-old Alice was in no rush to settle down.

Roosevelt was not discouraged. He told a friend, "See that girl? I'm going to marry her. She won't have me, but I am going to have her!"[4]

Roosevelt dated other women, but Alice was his favorite. They went out for over a year. Dates included dances and dinners. They took walks in winter snow and played tennis in summer. Finally, after much persuading, he won her heart.

On January 25, 1880, they became secretly engaged. Roosevelt was in his senior year of college. He wrote in his diary, ". . . after much pleading my own sweet, pretty darling consented to be my wife. Oh, how bewitchingly pretty she looked! If loving her with my whole heart and soul can make her happy, she shall be happy; . . ."[5]

Before the engagement was made public, the couple told their news to close friends and family. Included was young Edie Carow, the girl Roosevelt had known since he was seven. Roosevelt's sister Conie said that Edie was shocked and saddened by the news of the engagement.[6]

On February 14, the engagement was made public. Roosevelt was twenty-one and Alice was eighteen. At the time, it was considered important for a woman's father to offer his consent for his daughter to be married. Roosevelt thought Alice's father would say she was too young to marry. He believed her father would want a long engagement.

Mittie suggested that Roosevelt and Alice move into her house after they married. The suggestion was taken. Roosevelt told his sister, "Indeed, I don't think Mr. Lee would have consented to our marriage so soon on other terms."[7]

A wedding date was set for October. Meanwhile, Roosevelt still had to finish college. To graduate he had to write a senior essay. The theme he chose was women's equality. He expressed radical ideas for his time. Roosevelt wrote,

> . . . I think there can be no question that women should have the equal rights with men. . . . A son should have no more right to any inheritance than a daughter should have. . . . Especially as regards the laws relating to marraige (sic) there should be the most absolute equality preserved between the two sexes. I do not think the woman should assume the man's name.[8]

In spite of his busy schedule, Roosevelt took on another project in his last months at Harvard. He thought no decent history had been written about the War of 1812. Roosevelt decided to correct that by writing one himself.

While in college, Roosevelt became engaged to Alice Lee, shown here, holding the parasol.

The busy student also began to make plans for his future. He was accepted at Columbia University Law School in New York City. Law classes would start in the fall. Roosevelt also vowed to someday build a mansion in Oyster Bay and name it "Leeholm," in honor of Alice's family.

On June 30, 1880, Roosevelt graduated from Harvard. He ranked twenty-first in his class of 177 students.[9]

That summer, Roosevelt and his brother Elliott spent six weeks hunting in the Midwest. Upon his return, Roosevelt fulfilled his plan to enter Columbia Law School.

Although Alice had once been hesitant to settle down, she was now very much in love. On October 6, she wrote, "I should die without you now Teddy and there is not another man I ever could have loved in the whole world."[10]

The wedding took place on October 27, 1880, in Brookline, Massachusetts, outside Boston. It was warm for late October, a perfect fall day.

The couple took a quick honeymoon to Oyster Bay. They returned to New York City where Roosevelt attended classes. He also tried to fill his father's shoes by serving on the boards of charities. However, Roosevelt lost interest in both law school and charity work. He had another calling.

In the 1880s, most men of Roosevelt's wealth and background steered clear of politics. They felt politics attracted lowlifes and streetwise men. Roosevelt did not care. Politics was what he wanted.

He joined the Republican association in his district of the city and at age twenty-three was elected to the state assembly. A long political career had begun.

At the same time Roosevelt continued working on his book on the War of 1812. The research and writing were time-consuming and exhausting. When it was released, *The Naval War of 1812* was very well received. Roosevelt's second career as a writer had started.

As a state assemblyman, Roosevelt had to move to the state capital in Albany. Most of the time Alice stayed in New York with her mother-in-law, Mittie. As at Harvard, Roosevelt was first seen as peculiar by other assembly members. His fellow assemblymen wondered what this rich aristocrat was doing in politics. Also like the students at Harvard, they listened to Roosevelt's ideas and got to know him.

He made a reputation as a man hoping to clean up corruption in government. Many of his fellow assemblymen liked him for that. Others thought he acted morally superior, and looked down on him.[11]

Early on, Roosevelt's views were typical of those in his social class. He favored the rights of big business over workers and consumers. A man named Samuel Gompers helped change Roosevelt's mind.

Gompers headed a labor union representing cigar makers. Cigars were very popular, especially among the wealthy like the Roosevelts. Workers who made cigars for big tobacco companies were forced to do so in their crowded homes. A bill to outlaw this practice was being considered in the state assembly. Roosevelt planned to vote against it.

Gompers took Roosevelt into the slums where cigar makers worked. The young assemblyman was shocked and disgusted by what he saw. He described one home by saying, "There were several children, three men, and two women in this room. The tobacco was stowed about everywhere, alongside the foul bedding, and in a corner where there were scraps of food."[12]

Because of what he saw, Roosevelt changed his mind and voted in favor of the bill. From that point on, he was a champion of laborers' rights.

Early in 1882, there was some exciting news from another branch of the Roosevelt family. These Roosevelts lived about ninety miles north of New York City in the town of Hyde Park. Unlike Theodore Roosevelt's family, they were Democrats.

On January 30, 1882, distant cousins from Hyde Park, James and Sara Roosevelt, became parents. Sara gave birth to a baby boy, who was named Franklin.

In the summer of 1883, there was similar marvelous news in the Roosevelt home. Alice was pregnant. A baby was due in February 1884.

Near the end of summer, Theodore Roosevelt took advantage of a chance to hunt buffalo with friends in the Dakota Territory. (North and South Dakota were not states yet.) He enjoyed the hunt but missed Alice. While away he wrote, "I think all the time of my little, laughing, teasing beauty, and how pretty she is, and how she goes to sleep in my arms, and I could almost cry I love you so."[13]

In November, Roosevelt won a third one-year term in the state assembly. That fall and winter he and Alice made plans for the future. Roosevelt bought land in Oyster Bay where he hoped to build Leeholm, their dream house.

On February 12, 1884, Roosevelt was at work in Albany when he received word that Alice had given birth to a daughter. The new father was thrilled.[14]

The next morning he received a telegram stating that something was wrong with Alice. He boarded a train and headed home. The weather was dismal. Rain fell and the air was thick with fog. As the train arrived, Roosevelt exited and walked through the fog to his home.

Elliott answered the door. He said, "There is a curse on this house. Mother is dying and Alice is dying, too!"[15]

Mittie was suffering from typhoid, an illness caused by bad food or water. Alice had Bright's Disease, which attacks the kidneys. Alice had had the ailment throughout her pregnancy, but it was discovered too late. Alice was so sick she barely recognized her husband.

Mittie died in the early morning hours of February 14, Valentine's Day, 1884. Alice died later that same day. The baby survived and was christened Alice Lee

Roosevelt. The date was the fourth anniversary of the announcement of Roosevelt's engagement to Alice Lee.

Roosevelt wrote, "When my heart's dearest died, the light went from my life for ever."[16]

He never again brought up Alice's name.[17] Roosevelt was only willing to show his sensitive side in his private diary. It was there that he poured out his feelings. In those days, it was a sign of weakness for men to cry or discuss their emotions in public. When Roosevelt wrote his autobiography in 1913, he did not even mention Alice's name. It was as if she had never existed.

Roosevelt tried to cope by throwing himself into his work. Yet he was sorely depressed. A friend said, "He was in a stunned, dazed state. He does not know what he does or says."[18]

The only way Roosevelt could truly deal with his grief was to escape. When his term in the assembly expired, Roosevelt left baby Alice with his sister Bamie and left New York to make a new home in the Dakota Territory. He hoped to earn a living as a cattle rancher.

4

THE WILD WEST AND THE CIVIL EAST

The first impression Roosevelt gave the residents of the Dakota Territory was similar to the one he had given Harvard classmates and New York assemblymen. With his eastern accent and eyeglasses, he seemed out of place in the rugged West. Men like him were known among the cowboys as dudes. Because of his glasses, Roosevelt was called "Four-eyes."

He soon proved he could hold his own. It did not matter whether he was rounding up cattle or handling a bully. One time, Roosevelt was in a barroom when a drunken man with a gun in each hand began picking on him. The man said, "Four-eyes is going to treat," meaning Roosevelt would pay for everybody's drinks.[1]

Roosevelt acted as if the comment were a joke and laughed. The man with the guns was serious. He

followed Roosevelt around the barroom, swearing at him. Roosevelt played along and said, "Well, if I've got to, I've got to."[2]

In the old West, disputes were commonly settled with bullets and fists rather than words. Roosevelt stood up and punched the drunken man three times in the jaw. The man fell down senseless. This was hardly the same young Teedie who was tormented by two bullies on the stagecoach trip to Maine.

Roosevelt made his home in a log cabin on a ranch called the Maltese Cross. It had just three rooms. Yet for its time it was "luxurious."[3] Many other ranch cabins had only one room. There was even a desk on which Roosevelt wrote the manuscript for another book, *Hunting Trips of a Ranchman*. In it, he discussed life in the West:

> Though the ranchman is busiest during the round-up . . . he is far from idle at other times. He rides round among the cattle to see if any are sick, visits any outlying camp of his men, hunts up any bands of ponies which may stray—and they are always straying—superintends the haying, and, in fact, does not often find that he has too much leisure on his hands.[4]

Roosevelt's main goal was not simply to write. He hoped to earn money raising beef cattle. Still, he never forgot about politics. In September 1885 he returned home to attend the New York State Republican convention. He took time to visit baby Alice, in the care of Bamie. Roosevelt also saw his brother Elliott, and Elliott's baby daughter, Anna Eleanor. Anna Eleanor was born on October 14, 1884, and soon would be known simply as Eleanor. Roosevelt also visited his childhood friend, Edith Carow.

The house at Oyster Bay was now complete. Roosevelt had given Bamie permission to live in it with Alice. He, too, spent time there while home. In October, Roosevelt and Edith danced together at a ball at the mansion. Soon they were dating. On November 17, 1885, he asked her to marry him. She said yes.

Out of respect for his late wife Alice, Roosevelt asked that the engagement be kept secret for several months. He and Edith agreed to wait a year before marrying.

Roosevelt returned to his ranch home in the Dakota Territory. In 1886 there was a drought in the region. In addition, a surplus of cattle had caused beef prices to fall. Roosevelt left his herd of cattle in the care of his partners and returned to New York in September 1886. Except for a few short trips, he never lived on the ranch again.

The few years of strenuous work on the range finished the body-building job Roosevelt had started when he was eleven. By the time he was home for good, he was a mass of solid muscle and in peak condition.

Local Republicans asked Roosevelt to run for mayor of New York City. Known as the Cowboy Candidate, he ran against two strong candidates and finished third. He publicly said he was not disappointed.[5] Privately, he was very embarrassed to finish last.[6]

Following the election, Roosevelt and Edith were

Roosevelt married Edith Carow on December 2, 1886.

married on December 2, 1886, in New York City. The couple went on a four-month-long honeymoon in Europe. When they returned, they settled at the mansion in Oyster Bay.

Roosevelt dropped the idea of calling the house Leeholm. It was not fair to Edith that the house be named after his first wife's family. Instead, he called it Sagamore Hill. The name was in honor of Sagamore Mohannis, a Native American chief who lived on the land in the early 1600s.[7]

Bamie returned baby Alice to her brother and his new wife. Bamie later said, "It almost broke my heart to give her up. Still I felt . . . it was for her good, and that unless she lived with her father she would never see much of him."[8] Then, on September 12, 1887, Edith gave birth to a son. The boy was named Theodore Roosevelt, Jr. (When the future president was a child, he was known as Theodore, Jr. After the death of his father, he dropped the "Jr." from his name. So the new baby was named Theodore, Jr., instead of Theodore Roosevelt III.)[9]

Roosevelt continued writing. In 1888 he finished another book about his life in the Dakota Territory. It was called *The Winning of the West.*

In November 1888, a Republican, Benjamin Harrison, was elected President. After taking office, Harrison appointed Roosevelt civil service commissioner. He was to make certain that hiring for government jobs was done honestly. Many government jobs were given to a President's supporters whether or not they were qualified.

Roosevelt moved to Washington, D.C., in May 1889. The rest of the family joined him several months later. Roosevelt took his job very seriously and exposed people who accepted bribes and cheated on tests. He did such a thorough job that he became a small embarrassment for President Harrison. By uncovering case after case of fraud, he made it appear that the entire Harrison administration was corrupt.

Some members of the Republican "old guard" (older party members who had been in office for a long time) told Harrison to fire Roosevelt. Many supported Roosevelt, however. Most who did were a large group of moderate Republicans called Mugwumps. The word "mugwump" comes from a Native American word meaning "chieftain" or "big chief." It has come to mean any voter who thinks independently.

Harrison did not want to lose the Mugwumps' support. If he fired Roosevelt, it might anger them. So he asked Roosevelt in a diplomatic way to back off a bit. Roosevelt would have nothing of it. He proceeded with enthusiasm on his reform campaign.

At home, the Roosevelts were adding to their family. Another son, Kermit, was born in 1889. A daughter, Ethel Carow, was born two years later.

In 1892, Harrison ran for reelection, but lost to Democrat Grover Cleveland. (Cleveland had been elected President in 1884. He lost to Harrison in 1888, making him the only President to serve two nonconsecutive terms.) Cleveland kept Roosevelt on as civil service commissioner. In fact, Cleveland was more agreeable to reform than Harrison had been.

The Roosevelt family was getting even larger. In 1894, Edith gave birth to another boy, Archibald Bulloch Roosevelt. He would be called Archie. There was a sad event in the family that year, however. Roosevelt's brother Elliott died on August 14. His daughter Eleanor, now ten, was orphaned. (Her mother had died two years earlier.) She and a younger brother went to live with their grandmother.

During the summers, Eleanor visited Oyster Bay. Roosevelt took Eleanor under his wing. Because her parents had died, he felt sorry for her.[10] He tried to teach her to swim and took her on hikes with his children. Eleanor became her uncle Ted's favorite niece.[11]

As a result of Roosevelt's six years on the job, Americans greatly admired him as honest and hardworking. He also earned the respect of American women. Roosevelt enabled women to compete for federal jobs on the same level with men for the first time.

After six years Roosevelt was ready for something new. He returned to New York City in 1895 to become police commissioner. He was as aggressive in the police department as he was with the federal government. He promoted those who performed honest and quality work and dismissed those who took bribes or did not perform their jobs well. As before, Roosevelt tried to enforce laws as strictly as possible. Some citizens and politicians were annoyed by his eagerness.

In 1896 a Republican, William McKinley, was elected President. McKinley appointed Roosevelt assistant secretary of the Navy. Once more, he was off to Washington, D.C.

Roosevelt believed the United States Navy was weak. Some battleships dated from the Civil War. Roosevelt felt the Navy needed to be strengthened. His boss, Secretary of the Navy John D. Long, was a mild-mannered man. Roosevelt was so strong-willed that he practically dominated his boss.

The next year, the Roosevelts added to their family for the last time. A boy named Quentin was born on

By 1897, the Roosevelt family had a total of six children.

November 19, 1897. Life in the Roosevelt household was hectic, with six children ranging in age from infancy to thirteen years old.

It was also around this time that Roosevelt suffered his last asthma attack. Many people who suffer allergies or breathing problems outgrow them. Roosevelt was no different. (Unlike their father, none of the Roosevelt children had asthma.)

Although Roosevelt preferred peace to war, he believed in the glory of armed conflict. In 1897 he gave a speech at the Naval War College in Newport, Rhode Island, where he made a bold statement: "No triumph of peace is quite so great as the supreme triumphs of war."[12]

Throughout his life Roosevelt spoke highly of the virtue of fighting in war. His daughter Alice later said her father felt guilty because his father had avoided service in the Civil War.[13] Others said Roosevelt enjoyed the challenge of battle in the same way that he took pleasure in hunting. But he respected only honorable fighting. Historian John Gable said, "Roosevelt would never shoot anyone in the back."[14]

Soon there came a situation tailor-made for Roosevelt. In the late 1890s, the island nations of Cuba and the Philippines were under the rule of Spain. People of both countries were rebelling against Spanish rule. While the Philippine Islands are far away in the Pacific, Cuba is just ninety miles south of Florida.

In the 1890s the American frontier was declared

closed. That meant all the land in the West that could be developed had been settled. Many in the United States were hungry for more territory. Cuba seemed to be a logical spot for American expansion.

In January 1889, riots broke out in Cuba between rebels and Spanish officers. Because some Americans were living in Cuba, a warship named the U.S.S. *Maine* was sent there to protect them. Spain and the United States were technically at peace, so President McKinley called the visit "an act of friendly courtesy."[15] The *Maine* docked in Havana Harbor, in Cuba's capital of Havana. Then on February 15, 1898, disaster struck. The *Maine* exploded and 266 men were killed.[16]

The cause of the explosion was never discovered. It may have been an accident. Yet many did not want to believe that. They blamed the Spanish and wanted war. One of these people was Roosevelt. Their rallying cry was "Remember the *Maine*."

At first, McKinley would not declare war. Roosevelt complained that "McKinley has no more backbone than a chocolate eclair."[17]

In the days that followed, more and more Americans called for revenge against Spain. This included two powerful New York City newspapers, the *New York Journal* and the *New York World*. Soon, McKinley gave in to the demands and asked Congress for a declaration of war against Spain. On April 19, 1898, the declaration was approved by Congress.

Roosevelt was eager to prove himself. He resigned

his position as assistant secretary of the Navy and accepted a commission as a lieutenant colonel in a volunteer United States army. He would be second in command to a friend, an army surgeon named Leonard Wood.

So many men applied to serve with the regiment that only one in twenty was accepted.[18] Roosevelt chose men from many backgrounds. There were Jews, Irish, African Americans, and Anglo-Saxons. Some were wealthy Ivy League graduates while others were uneducated cowboys. This rough-and-tumble regiment became known as the Rough Riders.

Despite their differences, they were unified in a cause. Together they shouted the Rough Rider cheer: "Rough! tough! we're the stuff! We're the scrappers; never get enough! W-h-o-o-e-e!"[19] (The word "scrapper" meant a fighter.)

The Rough Riders soon got a chance to do some "scrapping." They landed in Cuba on June 22. Within days they were in the heat of battle. It was summer in the tropics. The temperature reached 100 degrees and it was brutally humid.

The Rough Riders suffered heavy losses in skirmishes as they approached two hills: Kettle Hill and San Juan Hill. Spanish forces were anchored on the summits of both hills. Beyond the hills was the city of Santiago. Its harbor was being held by Spain. If the Rough Riders could drive the Spanish from their bases on the hills, then the Spanish fleet at Santiago would be vulnerable.

SOURCE DOCUMENT

OATH OF OFFICE.

One to accompany the acceptance of every commissioned officer appointed or commissioned by the President in the Army of the United States.

I, Theodore Roosevelt, having been appointed a Colonel of the 1st U.S. Volunteer Cavalry in the military service of the United States, do solemnly swear (or affirm) that I will support and defend the Constitution of the United States against all enemies, foreign and domestic; that I will bear true faith and allegiance to the same; that I take this obligation freely, without any mental reservation or purpose of evasion; and that I will well and faithfully discharge the duties of the office on which I am about to enter: **So help me God.**

Theodore Roosevelt
Col 1st U.S.V. Cavalry

Sworn to and subscribed before me, at Camp Wikoff L.I., this 1st day of September, 1898.

H. G. Sprout
1st Lieut. 2nd Cav.
Judge Advocate G.C.M.

This is a copy of Theodore Roosevelt's oath of office for his appointment as colonel, in September 1898.

On July 1, 1898, Roosevelt, on horseback, led his troops, on foot, up Kettle Hill. The men fired their guns as they ran uphill. In the charge, Roosevelt's elbow was grazed by a bullet. Confronted by gun-wielding Rough Riders, the Spanish fled.

At the same time, United States troops were storming San Juan Hill. Roosevelt spotted them and called for his men to join the charge. Together, they all reached the summit. Again, the Spanish were overwhelmed and ran.

The Rough Riders did their job, but it was costly. They suffered the highest casualty rate of any regiment.[20] About 20 percent of the Rough Riders were killed or injured.[21]

On July 17, the United States Navy destroyed the Spanish fleet at Santiago. In August, the Navy, under Admiral George Dewey captured Manila in the Philippines. The Spanish-American War was over barely four months after it had started.

The United States was regarded as a world power for the first time. Roosevelt later wrote, "There are no four months of my life to which I look back with more pride and satisfaction."[22]

A popular man, Roosevelt was chosen to be the Republican nominee for governor of New York in 1898. With help from the Republican party boss, a man named Tom Platt, Roosevelt was elected. (A "party boss" is a person who has so much influence that he controls the actions of the entire party.)

This is Theodore Roosevelt as he appeared in his Rough Rider uniform when he led his troops in storming San Juan Hill.

Filled with as much fighting spirit as ever, Roosevelt again took on the role of reformer. In his one term of two years, he signed an amazing one thousand bills into law.[23] As before, Roosevelt helped pass laws that made sure government workers were hired on the basis of merit. Again, the old guard saw him as a troublemaker. When he signed a law taxing the profits of private corporations, he raised the anger of party boss Platt.

Platt decided Roosevelt should be removed as governor. The Vice President of the United States, Garret A. Hobart, had died in office in 1899. McKinley needed a new running mate. Platt thought that position would be a good place for Roosevelt. The Vice President has few real powers.

To the general public, Roosevelt was a hero. The charge up San Juan Hill was fresh in Americans' minds. In fact, it was becoming legendary. Stores sold Rough Rider board games and Rough Rider dolls. Campaign buttons featured images of Teddy Roosevelt, the Rough Rider hero.

In June 1900, the delegates at the Republican convention nominated Roosevelt to be McKinley's running mate. Not all Republicans were happy, though.

The national chairman of the Republican party was a businessman and United States senator from Ohio named Mark Hanna. Hanna strongly supported big business and opposed Roosevelt's reform ideas even more than Platt. Hanna exclaimed to his fellow

SOURCE DOCUMENT

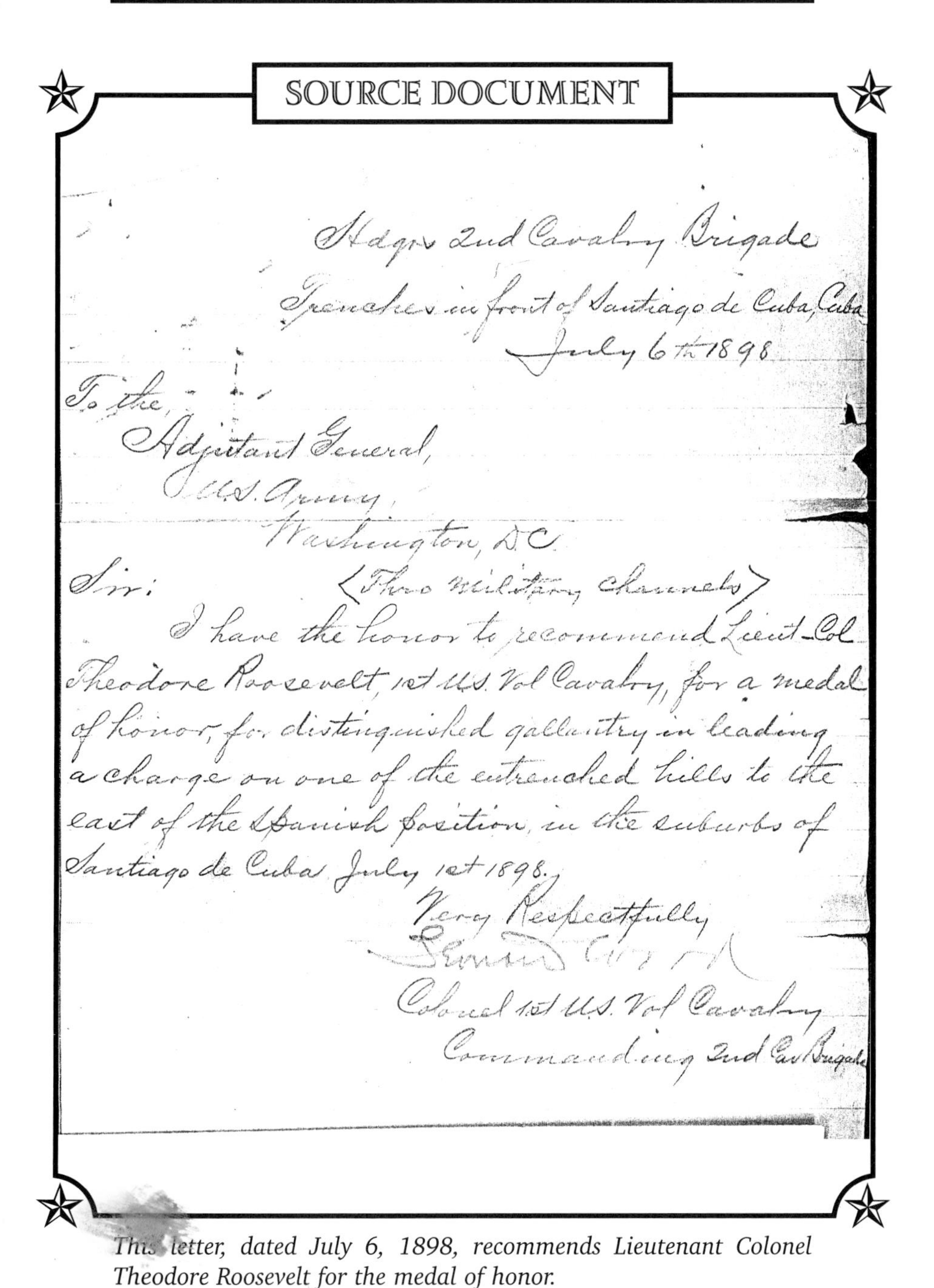

Hdqrs 2nd Cavalry Brigade
Trenches in front of Santiago de Cuba, Cuba
July 6th 1898

To the,
Adjutant General,
U.S. Army,
Washington, D.C.

Sir: (Thro military channels)

I have the honor to recommend Lieut-Col Theodore Roosevelt, 1st U.S. Vol Cavalry, for a medal of honor, for distinguished gallantry in leading a charge on one of the entrenched hills to the east of the Spanish position, in the suburbs of Santiago de Cuba July 1st 1898.

Very Respectfully
[illegible]
Colonel 1st U.S. Vol Cavalry
Commanding 2nd Cav Brigade

This letter, dated July 6, 1898, recommends Lieutenant Colonel Theodore Roosevelt for the medal of honor.

Republicans, "Don't any of you realize that there's only one life between this madman and the White House?"[24]

It did not seem to be a problem. McKinley was only fifty-seven years old and in good health when he was reelected in November 1900. When McKinley was inaugurated in March 1901, it appeared that Roosevelt was going to be buried in a powerless position for four years. Then President McKinley took a fateful trip to Buffalo, New York.

5

A STEAM-ENGINE IN TROUSERS

In 1901, Buffalo was home to a world's fair called the Pan-American Exposition. In the days before theme parks, world's fairs were major events. They took place in different cities in different years and people traveled hundreds of miles to attend them. The fairs had pavilions showing advancements in technology and the cultures of different countries. There are world's fairs today but they are not the major events they once were.

Because of the world's fair, Buffalo was an exciting place to be in 1901. Early September was an especially thrilling time. President McKinley planned a visit.

On September 6 at around 4:00 P.M., McKinley was at the World's Fair, shaking hands with the public. A young man named Leon F. Czolgosz (pronounced "chol-gosh") was waiting in line. Czolgosz was an anarchist.

Anarchists believe all forms of government are oppressive and should be abolished.

Czolgosz's right hand was covered with a handkerchief. It looked as if he had been in an accident. McKinley reached out to shake his left hand. As he did, Czolgosz shot McKinley at close range with a gun hidden under the handkerchief. McKinley was rushed to an emergency hospital on the world's fair grounds.

At the time, Roosevelt was in Vermont to give a speech. He was called to Buffalo, where he stayed for a few days. Since McKinley seemed to be recovering, Roosevelt was allowed to leave Buffalo.

Then McKinley took a turn for the worse. Doctors knew he would not live long. By then, Roosevelt was hiking with his family in the Adirondack Mountains, hundreds of miles away.

Roosevelt recalled,

> . . . I had descended a few hundred feet to a shelf of land where there was a little lake, when I saw a guide coming out of the woods on our trail from below. I felt at once that he had bad news, and, sure enough, he handed me a telegram saying that the President's condition was much worse and that I must come to Buffalo immediately.[1]

By the time Roosevelt arrived in Buffalo, McKinley was dead. On the evening of September 14, 1901, Roosevelt took the oath of office in the library of the home of a friend named Ansley Wilcox. As he concluded the oath, Roosevelt did not say the words, "So help me God." Those words were traditionally spoken by

Presidents taking the inaugural oath, beginning with George Washington. Instead Roosevelt said, "And thus I swear."[2]

The reason why Roosevelt ended the oath with his own words can only be guessed. Roosevelt believed strongly in the separation of church and state. Some historians say this might have been his way of applying his personal beliefs to the oath. Others say that since there was no Bible in the Wilcox library, Roosevelt did not feel right invoking the name of God.[3]

Czolgosz explained that he shot McKinley because he hated all rulers. It did not matter if they were kings or presidents. In a quick trial, Czolgosz was found guilty of killing McKinley. He was executed in the electric chair on October 29, just seven weeks after the shooting.

At age forty-two, Roosevelt was the youngest President in American history. He was also one of the most colorful. He stood only 5 feet 9 inches and had a stocky build, but was full of pep and energy. A United States senator named Joseph Foraker called him "a steam-engine in trousers."[4]

Roosevelt spoke with a high-pitched voice. While talking, he often used a fist to pound the palm of his other hand. He loved the adjective "bully." He used it to describe something fun he experienced. Today, people might say "excellent" or "awesome."

Some Americans were frightened that Roosevelt would get the nation into a war. Roosevelt shrugged that off with a joke. He responded, "What!, a war and I cooped up here in the White House? Never!"[5]

To make the American citizens feel at ease, Roosevelt kept McKinley's Cabinet. However, just a month after taking office, Roosevelt shocked the country. On October 16, he became the first President to invite an African American to dine in the White House. The guest was the well-known educator, Booker T. Washington.

Many residents of the South were outraged. It was just thirty-six years after the end of the Civil War. Many in the North as well as the South considered African Americans to be an inferior race. They found the event shocking.

In time Roosevelt proved in other ways that he was not William McKinley. To a degree, McKinley was a puppet of Mark Hanna and the interests of wealthy business owners. Roosevelt would be under the influence of no one except himself. In fact, when Roosevelt became President, Hanna is said to have exclaimed, "Now, look. That damned cowboy is President of the United States."[6]

Roosevelt soon proved to be the unfair businessmen's worst nightmare. He had nothing against big business. After all, his own family was wealthy. However, due to his father's example, he believed in fair and honest capitalism.

In honest capitalism, companies that provide services or make products are allowed to compete fairly.

The public (consumers) can do business with companies offering the best products or services at the fairest prices. Businesses and consumers both benefit.

Early in 1902, three major railroads in the West were under the control of one company. It was called the Northern Securities Company. (There were no airplanes then, and automobiles were just being developed. People and freight moved by train.) The company was owned by a partnership of men, but the kingpin was a millionaire named J. P. Morgan.

Because there was little competition, many companies shipping freight and many people traveling were forced to use trains owned by Morgan. Morgan was able to charge especially high prices, which he did.

The term for a company that allows no competition is a trust. A law was passed in 1890 which made unfair trusts illegal. It was called the Sherman Antitrust Act. Yet neither Presidents Harrison, Cleveland, nor McKinley enforced it. In fact, Roosevelt was to become the first President since Abraham Lincoln to truly use the full powers of his office.

Roosevelt said, "The government ought not to conduct the business of this country, but it ought to regulate it, so that it shall be conducted in the interest of the public."[7]

Roosevelt sued the Northern Securities Company on the grounds that it violated the Sherman Antitrust Act. He believed that the company should be broken up to allow for competition. Morgan was angry and visited

SOURCE DOCUMENT

From Roosevelt's first annual message to Congress, December 1901:

The captains of industry . . . have on the whole done great good to our people. Without them the material development of which we are so justly proud could never have taken place. . . . Yet it is also true that there are real and great evils. . . . There is a widespread conviction in the minds of the American people that the great corporations known as trusts are in certain of their features and tendencies hurtful to the general welfare. This . . . is based upon sincere conviction that combination and concentration should be, not prohibited, but supervised and within reasonable limits controlled; and in my judgment this conviction is right.

In his first annual message to Congress, President Roosevelt expressed his views on big business and the problem of trusts.

Roosevelt in the White House.[8] Morgan hoped to compromise, but Roosevelt would not do so. The case would be decided by a court of law.

Soon there was another chance for Roosevelt to take on a business giant. In May 1902, men working in the anthracite coal mines of Pennsylvania went on strike. They were represented by a union called the United Mine Workers (UMW). The UMW had several demands. These included safer working conditions, a forty-hour workweek, and a pay increase.

The mine owners refused to budge. They would not even recognize the UMW as the miners' official representative.

The man representing the owners was named George Baer. He was president of a company called Reading Iron & Coal. Baer summed up the owners' attitudes when he said the miners "don't suffer; why, they can't even speak English."[9] (Many of the miners were immigrants from eastern Europe.)

The strike continued through the summer and into the fall. Without the miners' work, coal supplies were dwindling across the country. In the early 1900s, millions of Americans used coal to heat their homes. Businesses, schools, and hospitals were also heated with coal. As winter was approaching, it seemed as if people would freeze without the means to heat the buildings where they lived and worked.

Roosevelt made attempts to bring the two sides together but with no luck. He was most frustrated with Baer and his hardened attitude. Roosevelt said of Baer, "If it wasn't for the high office I hold, I would have taken him by the seat of the breeches and the nape of the neck and chucked him out that window."[10]

With disaster on the horizon, Roosevelt made a daring move. He threatened to bring in federal troops to work the mines. Since that time, Presidents have made similar threats. But it was unheard of for a President to use such powers in 1902.

In October 1902, the mine owners agreed to have a panel help negotiate an end to the strike. The miners would return to work while a settlement was being decided.

The following March, the panel reached its decision. Workers' wages would be increased by 10 percent. Work days were reduced to either eight or nine hours. Severe abuses were corrected. A board was created to settle future differences. While the UMW was not formally recognized, its representatives were given seats on the panel.[11]

By now the American people knew they had a President who was not shy about using the powers of his office. He was seen by most as a man who used those powers to help the average American. The newspapers of the day referred to him by his initials, "TR." The public called him "Teddy," a name Roosevelt

In 1902, Roosevelt helped settle a strike in the coal mines of Pennsylvania. He is shown here with a group of coal miners.

never really cared for.[12] Whatever he was called, Theodore Roosevelt was viewed as a champion of the common people.

Soon another incident turned Roosevelt into a folk hero. He was in Mississippi in 1902 on a bear hunt. Since he was having poor luck, his hosts captured an old bear and tied it to a tree. Roosevelt would have an easy target and not go home empty-handed.

The President refused to shoot the bear. He said killing a captive animal went against the code of good sportsmanship. The bear was set free. A newspaper cartoonist named Clifford Berryman drew a cartoon about Roosevelt's decision. In New York City, a toy maker named Morris Michtom decided to craft a small stuffed bear and call it a teddy bear in honor of the President. In no time, the children of America were buying teddy bears. They still do nearly one hundred years later.

As a result of his conflicts with the railroad and mining industries, Roosevelt decided a new Cabinet position was needed. In 1903, he convinced Congress to authorize the Department of Commerce and Labor. Its main purpose was to regulate business so companies could compete fairly.

As President, Roosevelt had the chance to build up the Navy as he had always wished to do. He convinced Congress that the Navy's fleet was outdated. Congress agreed with him. Each year that he was President, Roosevelt was able to persuade Congress to authorize at least one new battleship for the Navy. Congress authorized five ships in 1903 alone.

Away from work, Roosevelt practiced what he called "the strenuous life."[13] For recreation he led family and guests on so-called point-to-point hikes. During these hikes, one was allowed to walk over, under, or through—but never around—any obstacle. Some were taken in Rock Creek Park in Washington. Others were taken in the woods around Sagamore Hill.

Once, Roosevelt led the French ambassador on a point-to-point hike. When they came to a creek, Roosevelt said they would have to swim across it. He undressed and made his guest do so, too. The President and ambassador then swam naked across the creek. A British diplomat named Cecil Spring Rice said, "You must always remember that the President is about six [years old]."[14] Perhaps the adult Theodore Roosevelt was making up for the childhood that young, sickly Teedie could never really enjoy.

Roosevelt felt all Americans should have access to the joys of the outdoors as he did. By the end of the 1800s, more than half of the country's timber had been cut.[15] Roosevelt believed this trend must be stopped.

He appointed a man named Gifford Pinchot to head the United States Forest Service. Roosevelt and Pinchot fought Congress and industrialists to add 150 million acres to the nation's protected forest land. Roosevelt also established fifty wild game preserves, five national parks, and sixteen national monuments.[16] The most famous of the national monuments is the Grand Canyon. Today it is a national park.

In a speech at the Grand Canyon in 1903, Roosevelt said,

> Leave it as it is. You cannot improve on it; not a bit. The ages have been at work on it, and man can only mar it. What you can do is to keep it for your children, your children's children and for all who come after you, as one of the great sights which every American, if he can travel at all, should see.[17]

6

THE BIG STICK

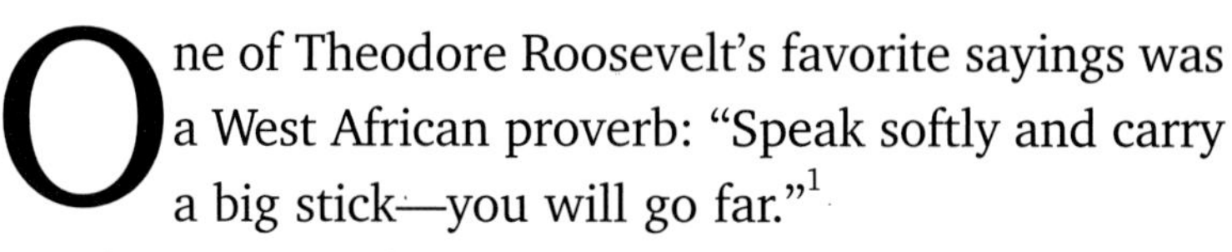

One of Theodore Roosevelt's favorite sayings was a West African proverb: "Speak softly and carry a big stick—you will go far."[1]

The "speak softly" part of the proverb means to use diplomacy in trying to accomplish what you think is right. The "carry a big stick" part means to be able to back up your position with force if necessary.

Roosevelt used that proverb as a basis for his dealings with the mine owners during the coal strike of 1902. In 1903, he applied it to foreign policy.

People had dreamed for years of building a canal through Central America. Ships sailing from the Atlantic to the Pacific Ocean had to travel around the tip of South America. That made for lengthy and costly voyages. A canal through Central America would save much time and money.

A French company tried building a canal through Panama in Central America in 1878. Panama was not an independent country then as it is today. It was part of the South American nation of Colombia. The French company did not manage its finances well and suffered technical setbacks. The project was stopped, unfinished, in 1889.

Another French company took over and offered to sell its equipment and the rights to the job to the United States in 1903. The United States Senate and House of Representatives approved the sale. For the deal to be completed, Colombia had to agree to sell enough land for canal construction to the United States.

Roosevelt said he believed in using diplomacy to get things done, but he knew it was important to back up decisions with strength.

At first, Colombia agreed to a price. Then they asked for more money. When Roosevelt agreed to a new price, they asked for even more money. Roosevelt grew more and more frustrated.[2]

Meanwhile, the people of Panama had long been unhappy with the leadership of the government of Colombia. Many wanted independence. They took part in several rebellions against the Colombian government. Roosevelt counted fifty-three uprisings in the preceding fifty-three years.[3]

On November 5, 1903, another revolt took place. A group of Panamanian military leaders took control of Panama and declared independence from Colombia. On November 9, Roosevelt officially recognized the new independent country of Panama. American warships were sent to Panama to keep the Colombian military away. Within a week, Panama and the United States agreed on a contract to build the canal. By the middle of 1904, work had begun.

Historians today debate whether Roosevelt did anything to stir up the revolt. A few say he had a direct hand in it. Most say he did nothing to encourage the revolt, but did nothing to stop it once it had started.[4]

Roosevelt was proud of his quick action in arranging the deal with Panama. Some years later he said,

> If I had followed traditional methods, I should have submitted a dignified state paper of probably two hundred pages to the Congress, and the debate would have been going on yet. But I took the Canal Zone and let Congress debate. And while the debate goes on, the canal does also.[5]

SOURCE DOCUMENT

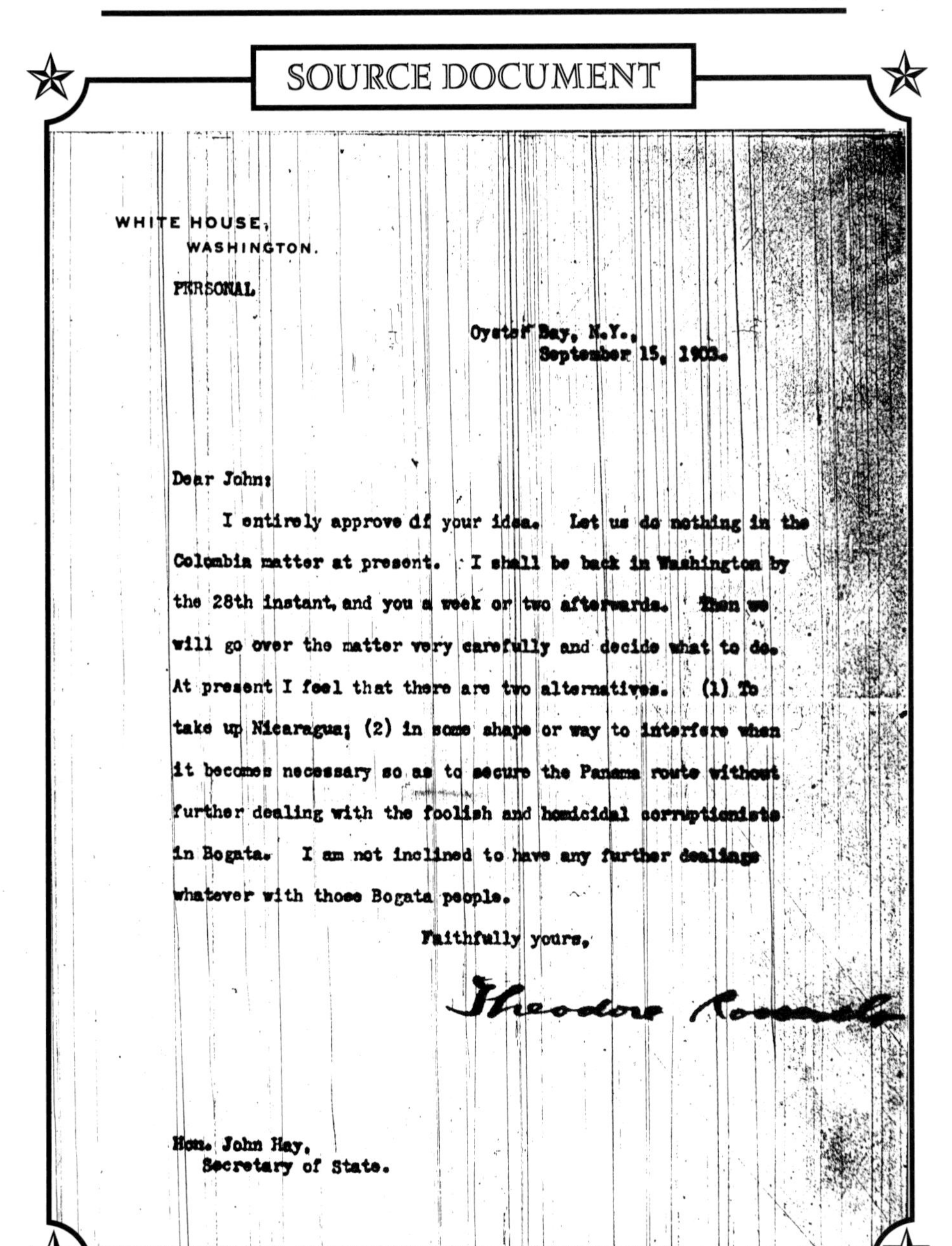

WHITE HOUSE,
WASHINGTON.

PERSONAL

Oyster Bay, N.Y.,
September 15, 1903.

Dear John:

I entirely approve of your idea. Let us do nothing in the Colombia matter at present. I shall be back in Washington by the 28th instant, and you a week or two afterwards. Then we will go over the matter very carefully and decide what to do. At present I feel that there are two alternatives. (1) To take up Nicaragua; (2) in some shape or way to interfere when it becomes necessary so as to secure the Panama route without further dealing with the foolish and homicidal corruptionists in Bogata. I am not inclined to have any further dealings whatever with those Bogata people.

Faithfully yours,

Theodore Roosevelt

Hon. John Hay,
Secretary of State.

In this letter, dated September 15, 1903, Theodore Roosevelt expresses his interest in Secretary of State John Hay's ideas about building the Panama Canal.

The year 1904 was an election year. Roosevelt would be running for a term as President in his own right. Because he became President after the death of McKinley, some viewed him as an accidental President. Those who did not like Roosevelt called him "His Accidency."[6]

In March 1904, the United States Supreme Court ruled on Roosevelt's lawsuit against J. P. Morgan's railroad monopoly. Five of the nine judges ruled that Morgan's company had violated the Sherman Antitrust Act. Roosevelt had won, the monopoly was dissolved.

Overall, Roosevelt was well liked. The American people admired his energetic style and his policies. In fact, his whole family was popular. In 1904, the Roosevelt children ranged in age from six to twenty. There had not been small children in the White House since Abraham Lincoln was President.

The Roosevelt kids and their friends were known as the "White House Gang."[7] They were typically mischievous young people. They thought nothing of taking trays from the pantry and sliding down the White House stairs. They tossed water balloons on members of the Secret Service. Once, they pelted an oil painting of President Andrew Jackson with spitballs, and were duly punished.

Much of the time, the President enjoyed acting like a child when he was with his children. He had pillow fights and ran obstacle races with them. He also played hide-and-seek, and loved being "it."

SOURCE DOCUMENT

WHITE HOUSE,
WASHINGTON. June 22d
1904

Darling Ethel,

Here goes for the picture letter!

Ethel administers necessary discipline to Archie and Quentin.

Theodore Roosevelt's sense of humor and affection for his family are evident in this picture letter he wrote to his daughter Ethel.

The children had all sorts of pets. There were not only cats and dogs, but badgers, raccoons, guinea pigs, snakes, and a pony named Algonquin. One day young Quentin dumped three live snakes in his father's lap during a meeting with the attorney general. Another time Archie was sick in bed with the measles. Quentin thought Algonquin might cheer up his brother. So he talked a White House coachman into helping him bring the pony into Archie's room. They did so, by way of the White House elevator.[8] A White House butler named Ike Hoover said, "A nervous person had no business around the White House in those days."[9]

Edith Roosevelt was a popular First Lady. As did most First Ladies of that day, she served as official White House hostess. She planned receptions, dinners, and teas for diplomats and other guests. In addition, she was respected for her intelligence. She could hold her own when talking with important visitors such as Booker T. Washington.

When not hosting gatherings, Edith aided her husband in his duties as president. She helped sort his mail, reviewed official papers prepared by staff members, and when asked by her husband, offered advice. She appeared to be very good at that. A reporter named Mark Sultan said of the President, "Never, when he had his wife's judgment, did he go wrong or suffer disappointment."[10]

Edith also arranged for a complete renovation of the White House. When Roosevelt took office, the grand old building was in need of repair. In addition, the design was out of style for its time. Under Edith's direction, the White House was strengthened and decorated in a more modern style.

It was under Roosevelt that the President's home became officially known as the White House. Although most Americans called it the White House, its official name was the Executive Mansion. Roosevelt issued an executive order changing the formal name to the White House.

When the Roosevelts were not in Washington, the

SOURCE DOCUMENT

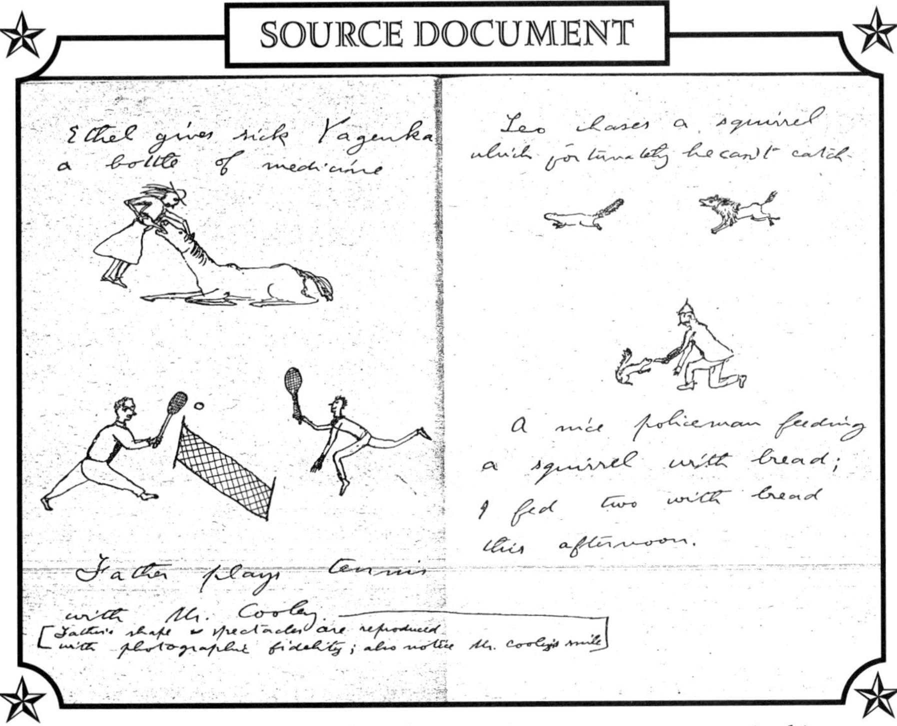

Ethel gives sick Yagenka a bottle of medicine

Father plays tennis with Mr. Cooley.

[Father's shape & spectacles are reproduced with photographic fidelity; also notice Mr. Cooley's smile]

Leo chases a squirrel which fortunately he can't catch.

A nice policeman feeding a squirrel with bread; I fed two with bread this afternoon.

Roosevelt's love of animals and interest in sports are apparent in this picture letter he wrote to his children.

The Roosevelt children kept many pets, including the pony, Algonquin, who Quentin Roosevelt (seated on pony) once brought inside the White House.

press followed them to Sagamore Hill to report on their activities. Alice especially pleased reporters looking for a good story. In 1904 she was twenty years old. She was an independent young woman and was very lovely to look at.

Women were expected to behave in certain ways then. For example, it was improper for a woman to travel or even drive a car on her own. An adult was supposed to supervise any couple on a date. In addition, proper women never drank, smoked, or gambled.

Alice enjoyed shocking people by breaking these

unwritten rules. Alice drove a car and smoked cigarettes in public. (This was long before cigarettes were proven to be harmful to one's health.) She was spotted paying money to a bookmaker at horse races.[11] (A bookmaker, or bookie, is a person who places bets for people.) Once, while cruising in the Pacific, she jumped into the ship's pool with her clothes on.[12]

Some of the public loved Alice's independence. Others found it disgraceful. The press was fascinated by her every move. They called her "Princess Alice." One day, the President was in a meeting with a friend in the White House. Alice kept entering the room and interrupting the meeting. The friend asked the President, "Theodore, isn't there anything you can do to control Alice?"

Roosevelt responded, "I can do one of two things. I can be President of the United States or I can control Alice. I cannot possibly do both."[13]

Of all the Roosevelt children, Quentin was perhaps the family favorite.[14] Roosevelt's grandson, Tweed, later said, "Quentin in many ways had the most promise. And in many ways he was so like his father that TR, I think, thought that Quentin might well be the one that followed in his footsteps."[15]

Roosevelt was elected to his own term as President in November 1904 in a landslide. The Democratic nominee was Alton Parker, a New York judge.

Roosevelt later wrote with pride, "I won by popular majority of about two million and a half, and in the

Edith Roosevelt was a popular First Lady, who helped her husband with many of his presidential duties.

electoral college carried 330 votes against 136. It was by far the largest popular majority ever hitherto given any presidential candidate."[16]

Immediately Roosevelt said he would not run for another term in 1908. Legally he could have. However, he wished to continue the tradition of no more than two terms for any President. Although his first term was only three and a half years, he considered it a full term. (In 1951, the Twenty-second Amendment was added to the United States Constitution. It limits all Presidents to a maximum of two terms.)

Just one month later, Roosevelt addressed Congress and referred to an earlier President, James Monroe. In 1823 Monroe proclaimed that the United States would protect the established countries of North and South America. In other words, if a European country actively meddled in a Western Hemisphere country's affairs, that would be recognized as a cause for war. This proclamation is called the Monroe Doctrine.

In Roosevelt's speech, he made the Monroe Doctrine even stronger. He said that, to maintain stability in the Western Hemisphere, the United States would take action if a European country interfered even slightly in a Latin American country's private affairs. Roosevelt said the United States would be assuming the position of an "international police power."[17] This is known as the Roosevelt Corollary. (A corollary is an action or statement that naturally follows one that already exists.)

In February 1905, the United States put Roosevelt's words into action. An island country in the Caribbean Sea called Santo Domingo was not repaying money it owed to countries in Europe. (Santo Domingo is now the Dominican Republic.) Roosevelt was concerned that these European nations would try to collect the money by force.

Unrest in Santo Domingo might have spilled over into Panama and disrupted the building of the canal. With permission from the president of Santo Domingo, Roosevelt sent Americans there to take over their customs office. (A customs office oversees imports and exports.) Americans remained in control of Santo Domingo for two years.

SOURCE DOCUMENT

Chronic wrongdoing, or an impotence which results in a general loosening of the ties of civilized society, may in America, as elsewhere, ultimately require intervention by some civilized nation, and in the Western Hemisphere the adherence of the United States to the Monroe Doctrine may force the United States, however reluctantly, in flagrant cases of such wrongdoing or impotence, to the exercise of an international police power.

This excerpt from the Roosevelt Corollary illustrates President Roosevelt's belief that the Monroe Doctrine of American influence in the Western Hemisphere should be strengthened.

Roosevelt was inaugurated for a second term as President on March 4, 1905. Less than two weeks later, on March 17, he had a family affair to attend. His niece Eleanor was marrying her distant cousin, Franklin Roosevelt. Since Eleanor's father was dead, Theodore Roosevelt took on the traditional role of the father of the bride and gave Eleanor away at the wedding.

Roosevelt said to the groom, "Well, Franklin, there's nothing like keeping the name in the family."[18]

That summer was when President Roosevelt helped negotiate a settlement to the Russo-Japanese War. In the fall, Roosevelt turned his attentions to the activities on another battlefront: the American gridiron.

In the early 1900s, there was no National Football League (NFL). The only game was college football. It was very popular, but also dangerous. Uniforms at the time offered little protection and there were hardly any rules to guard players from injury. Many players broke the few existing rules without suffering penalties. In the 1905 season, twenty-three men died playing football.[19] Some colleges banned football altogether.

Roosevelt loved the game when played fairly. He once wrote in a magazine article for children, "in life, as in a football game, the principle to follow is: Hit the line hard; don't foul and don't shirk, but hit the line hard!"[20]

Roosevelt decided that football must be reformed if it were to survive. On October 9, 1905, he met with six coaches and advisors in the White House. Together,

Roosevelt was concerned that the uniforms worn by football players did not offer enough protection against the unnecessary violence of the game. He worked to help reform the game of football.

they made a public statement condemning unneeded violence.

As a result of the meeting, the National Collegiate Athletic Association (NCAA) was formed. New rules were set. One allowed the forward pass. Another set ten yards as a goal for a first down. (It had been five yards.) The rules opened up the game and spread the players further around the field. That made for fewer chances for cheap violence.

Other news came out of the White House that fall. Alice was dating the speaker of the house, a Republican congressman from Ohio named Nicholas Longworth. The two were married in a lavish White House wedding on February 17, 1906. Cousin Eleanor could not attend, however. She was pregnant with her first child. Pregnant women of Eleanor's social class were not seen in public then.

Politically, Roosevelt continued his activist policies. He compared his approach to an honest card game. He called it "the Square Deal." This meant that every person was dealt a fair shake in life.

Roosevelt explained, "I stand for fair play and I stand for a square deal. Ours is a government of liberty. No man is above it. No man is below it. We must treat each man on his worth and merits as a man. Each is entitled to no more and no less."[21]

As part of the Square Deal, Roosevelt pressed Congress to pass the Hepburn Act. This law further regulated railroads. Around the same time he convinced

Roosevelt (right) is shown here at the wedding of his daughter, Alice, to Nicholas Longworth in 1906.

Congress to pass the Pure Food and Drug Act and the Meat Inspection Act. These made it illegal for food companies to ship unfit and unsafe foods. They also called for honest labels for packaged foods.

A novel by an author named Upton Sinclair helped spur on these laws. The book was called *The Jungle.* It described horrible working conditions in the meat packing industry.

A famous writer named Jack London wrote, ". . . what *Uncle Tom's Cabin* did for black slaves, *The Jungle* has a large chance to do for the white slaves of today . . ."[22]

Sinclair was one of a group of writers Roosevelt called muckrakers. In addition to Sinclair, some of the more famous included Ida Tarbell, Ray Stannard Baker, and Lincoln Steffens. The muckrakers wrote about corruption in high places, such as in business and politics.

Although Roosevelt was a reformer, he thought some muckrakers went too far. He said some attacked honest people whose only sin was being wealthy. At the same time, he stressed that fair investigative writers were doing a public good.[23] Regardless, the muckrakers went on uncovering what they considered to be corruption.

Roosevelt did not succeed in all his attempts to reform what he felt was wrong. An activist named John Spargo wrote a book in 1906 called *The Bitter Cry of the Children.* It uncovered details about children hired to work in mines and factories. Many had jobs that were

SOURCE DOCUMENT

From Upton Sinclair's *The Jungle*:

This is no fairy story and no joke; the meat would be shoveled into carts, and the man who did the shoveling would not trouble to lift out a rat even when he saw one—there were things that went into the sausage in comparison with which a poisoned rat was a tidbit. There was no place for the men to wash their hands before they ate their dinner, and so they made a practice of washing them in the water that was to be ladled into the sausage. There were the butt-ends of smoked meat, and the scraps of corned beef, and all the odds and ends of the waste of the plants, that would be dumped into old barrels in the cellar and left there. Under the system of rigid economy which the packers enforced, there were some jobs that it only paid to do once in a long time, and among these was the cleaning out of the waste barrels. Every spring they did it; and in the barrels would be dirt and rust and old nails and stale water—and cart load after cart load of it would be taken up and dumped into the hoppers with fresh meat, and sent out to the public's breakfast.

Upton Sinclair's words helped spur Congress to pass the Meat Inspection Act.

cruel even for adults. Yet hiring children was perfectly legal.

Spargo described boys nine or ten years old working in coal mines.

> From the cramped position they have to assume, most of them become more or less deformed and bent-backed like old men . . . The coal is hard, and accidents to the hands, such as cut, broken, or crushed fingers, are common among the boys.[24]

He also discussed girls who worked in textile mills. Spargo wrote of one girl,

> All day long, in a room filled with clouds of steam, she has to stand barefooted in pools of water twisting coils of wet hemp. When I saw her she was dripping wet . . . In the coldest evenings of winter little Marie, and hundreds of other little girls, must go out from the super-heated steaming rooms into the bitter cold in just that condition. No wonder that such children are stunted and underdeveloped![25]

The public and Roosevelt were shocked by what Spargo wrote. Roosevelt said, "The government should do away with the evils of child labor. It is not only a disgrace to the community, but a reproach to the American public."[26]

However, wealthy business owners had huge influence over the members of Congress. They did not want to see an end to child labor, since children were paid lower wages than adults. Roosevelt was able to get just one minor law passed. It banned child labor in Washington, D.C. This was an empty victory because very little child labor existed there.

In 1906, Roosevelt once more showed his open-mindedness. He named the first Jewish person, Oscar Straus, to a Cabinet position, the secretary of the Department of Commerce and Labor.

In November 1906, Roosevelt made a different kind of history. He left Washington to inspect the progress in building the Panama Canal. Roosevelt was the first President ever to leave the United States while in office.[27]

7

THE TWILIGHT YEARS

The last stretch of Roosevelt's presidency was starting on a sour note. In December 1906, Roosevelt gave a controversial message to Congress. In it he suggested the strongest controls yet on big business. These included forcing all companies to open their financial records so the public and the government could inspect them. Business owners were outraged.

About the same time, there were rumors that the stock market was weakening. By mid-March 1907, the stock market started to collapse. Over the course of a week, large numbers of anxious stockholders sold their stocks. As a result, the values of the stocks of major companies dropped sharply. No banks were forced to close, but Americans were nervous about the future. Workers might be given pay cuts or even lose their jobs.

On the other side of the world, there was strong anti-American feeling in Japan. This was in spite of the fact that Roosevelt had brought peace between Japan and Russia.

Some Japanese citizens thought their country was cheated in the Treaty of Portsmouth. In addition, they were most outraged by a ruling of the school board in San Francisco, California, in October 1906. Thousands of Japanese immigrants lived in California. Most were in San Francisco, where schools were highly overcrowded. To ease the situation, the school board pulled all Japanese children out of established public schools. They would be sent to segregated schools, along with Chinese and Korean children.

Roosevelt was angered by this racist law.[1] He stated that Japanese Americans were entitled to the same rights as other Americans. He even threatened to call out the National Guard to protect all citizens of California.[2]

On February 9, 1907, Roosevelt met at the White House with the mayor of San Francisco and other officials. They reached an agreement. Japanese-American children would be allowed to attend the same schools as white children. However, Japan would have to agree to cut back sharply on the number of immigrants entering the United States. Japan agreed to limit emigration. Since this was not a formal treaty, it was known as a "gentlemen's agreement."

It proved to be a total failure. Japanese children did

return to schools with whites in San Francisco. Some white adults were angry about this. In May and June of 1907, white mobs there attacked Japanese businessmen. Meanwhile, Japan did not reduce immigration to the United States.

Talk of war between Japan and the United States was heating up. It was time for Roosevelt to bring out the "big stick." To show Japan the strength of the American military, he ordered a huge fleet of United States Navy ships on an around-the-world cruise. All the ships were painted white. This American armada was known as the Great White Fleet.

While the Great White Fleet was preparing for its departure, the economy at home was shaky. Some days the stock market rallied. Other times it weakened. On August 7 prices collapsed to the same level they had been in the middle of March.

Things got worse by October. Many people were afraid their banks would go out of business. If that happened, the people would lose all their money. So they rushed to their banks to withdraw their savings. That forced some banks to close. If this trend continued, even more banks would close. That would mean severe trouble for the country's economy.

On October 23, the situation was on the brink of disaster. Roosevelt was on a hunting trip in Louisiana. Upon hearing the bad news, he rushed back to Washington. His secretary of the treasury, George Cortelyou, deposited $25 million of government money into banks in New York to keep them from going out of business. To help out, a rich businessman put another $25 million in an important bank called the Trust Company of America. The businessman was J. P. Morgan, Roosevelt's old rival. The banks survived.

This economic scare is known as the Panic of 1907. In some ways, it turned out to be a blessing in disguise. Because the panic showed that faults existed in the banking system, laws to improve it were passed in 1908. More laws were passed over the next several years.

Soon afterward, Roosevelt's Great White Fleet was ready to depart. On December 16, sixteen battleships left the coast of Virginia. Roosevelt stood on the presidential yacht, *Mayflower,* and watched the ships pass by. He was thrilled by the display of power. He called out, "Did you ever see such a fleet and such a day? By George, isn't it magnificent!"[3]

Roosevelt was determined to show the world the naval strength of the United States. He had done much to build it. In 1901 the United States Navy ranked fifth among the world's nations. By 1907, it was second only to Great Britain.[4]

Officially, the massive voyage was done in the name of friendship. Japan's Admiral Heihachiro Togo was agreeable. "We will greet the men as friends," Togo announced.[5]

The fleet's first stops were in South America. In honor of the fleet, there were parties and receptions in Rio de Janeiro, Brazil. The ships were not scheduled to visit Argentina for lack of time. Argentina's leaders persisted, however, and won a stop by the Americans. In Peru, there was a similar rousing welcome.

Roosevelt kept his promise not to run for reelection. He wanted his secretary of war, William Howard Taft, as his successor. He believed Taft would continue the policies of reform that Roosevelt had supported for nearly eight years. Roosevelt worked hard so that Taft would receive the Republican nomination for President in 1908.

Opponents said Taft was little more than a puppet of Roosevelt. A popular joke at the time was that the letters in the name T.A.F.T. stood for "Take Advice From Theodore."[6]

Roosevelt was still a much-loved man in his country. By the middle of 1908, the economy had improved. In addition, the world tour of the Navy was a success. Roosevelt could have run for another term as President and likely been elected.

The Republican National Convention was held in June in Chicago. Taft was supposed to be the star of the convention, but he was overshadowed by Roosevelt. The evening before Taft was to be nominated, a large number of delegates started a rally in favor or Roosevelt. They marched around the convention hall for nearly fifty minutes shouting, "four more years, four more years."[7]

Taft was nominated on the first ballot. However, the reception given to him was quiet compared to

SOURCE DOCUMENT

Private

Oyster Bay, N.Y.,
September 20, 1907.

Dear Murray:

I was sorry not to see you, as there is much to talk about. For some time I have been sure that we were going to have a period of contraction in business. The utter recklessness of the financial world, and the worse than recklessness of its most eminent leaders, the Rockefellers, Harrimans, and the like, rendered this absolutely inevitable. The trouble that they are now having over copper, the trouble that they have had over the Interborough Railroad, are perfectly typical of the business operations that have done most to bring about the revulsion. I am inclined to doubt whether there will be anything like a panic, and of course no one can say exactly how far things will go. There is one thing that I can say, however. The Post, Times, Sun, Harper's Weekly, and all the rest of the papers that find their inspiration among the worst elements of Wall Street, may as well make up their minds that the policies for which I stand have come to stay. Not only will they not change them, but in their es-

President Roosevelt's presidency faced rough times during the Panic of 1907. In this letter, dated September 20, 1907, Roosevelt writes to

sence they will not be changed by any man that comes after me, unless the reactionaries should have their way and produce a temporary reversal, in which case we should see a far more drastic and therefore undesirable action after the brief period of reaction had spent itself. I am amused at the shortsighted folly of the very wealthy men, and I am deeply concerned to find out how large a proportion of them stand for what is fundamentally corrupt and dishonest. Every year that I have lived has made me a firmer believer in the plain people - in the men who gave Abraham Lincoln his strength - and has made me feel more distrust of the over-educated dilettante type for whom the Evening Post speaks, and above all, the plutocratic type represented by the Sun, Times and the rest; and in my judgment the one way in which we can be absolutely certain of having bad times is to have the Republican party undertake to revise the tariff next winter. If we had meddled with the tariff before this we should have had bad times already. If we escape a panic now, as I hope and believe we shall, the check will be ultimately a benefit; and then, immediately after the next election, I think the Republican party should undertake the revision - not that there is any great need of it, but because public sentiment demands it.

Sincerely yours,

President Nicholas Murray Butler,
Columbia University,
New York.

Columbia University President Nicholas Murray Butler about the country's economic troubles.

Roosevelt's. The Democrats nominated William Jennings Bryan. Bryan had run for President in 1896 and 1900 and lost both times.

Throughout the summer and fall of 1908, the Great White Fleet received warm welcomes in the Pacific. On August 20, it arrived at Sydney, Australia. The Australians happily greeted it. The next stop was Manila, in the Philippines. Finally, on October 19, the fleet docked in Tokyo, Japan.

A total of two thousand Japanese children greeted the sailors, waving American flags and singing "The Star-Spangled Banner." Japanese and American ships saluted each other with ceremonial gun blasts. At night, electric lights were shaped in letters that spelled out a welcome to the visiting United States sailors. As Admiral Togo had promised, the Americans were greeted as friends.

Just two weeks later, the United States held its presidential election. Taft overwhelmingly defeated Bryan. He received over a million more popular votes. He also won the electoral college, 321 votes to 162.[8] Roosevelt gloated, "We have beaten them to a frazzle!"[9]

On February 22, 1909, the Great White Fleet returned home to Norfolk, Virginia. Roosevelt later wrote, "In my own judgment the most important service that I rendered to peace was the voyage of the battle fleet round the world."[10]

Others disagreed. Roosevelt's critics considered the world voyage to be a show of "gunboat diplomacy." That meant they felt Roosevelt was trying to keep other countries in line by showing off the United States' military might.

Just ten days after the fleet returned, William Howard Taft was inaugurated as the twenty-seventh President of the United States. Roosevelt retired to private life. He was just fifty years old. The vast majority of United States Presidents were over fifty when they first took office.

8

THE BULL MOOSE

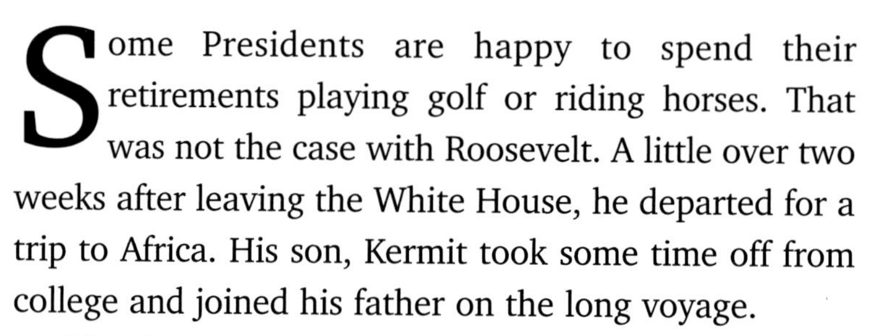

Some Presidents are happy to spend their retirements playing golf or riding horses. That was not the case with Roosevelt. A little over two weeks after leaving the White House, he departed for a trip to Africa. His son, Kermit took some time off from college and joined his father on the long voyage.

The journey was sponsored by the Smithsonian Institution. The Smithsonian is a complex of museums owned by the federal government. Most are in Washington, D.C. Roosevelt and Kermit would hunt wild animals. The Smithsonian would study them and turn some into museum exhibits.

Much of Africa today consists of modern cities with up-to-date facilities. In 1909, Africa was mostly unexplored and wild. Some people in the United States feared for Roosevelt's safety.

New York City political boss Tom Platt said, "There are a great many people who do not think Mr. Roosevelt will ever return from Africa alive. Many who have undertaken the same trip have been stricken by disease or killed by accident. He is taking a long chance."[1]

Both Roosevelts survived the trip, which was the most successful scientific expedition ever made to Africa at that time.[2] It lasted a total of eleven months. During that time, the two men shot and killed over five hundred animals.[3] The list included everything from zebras to pythons.

As usual, Roosevelt put his experiences into writing. He first wrote about his adventures for a magazine

Theodore Roosevelt is shown here with a dead rhinocerous, one of the many animals he shot on his African trip.

called *Scribner's.* Then he wrote a book called *African Game Trials.* Roosevelt described an elephant hunt this way:

> The cover was so high that we could not see their tusks, only the tops of their heads and their backs being visible. Their leader was the biggest, and at it I fired when it was sixty yards away, and nearly broadside on, but heading slightly toward me. I previously warned every one to kneel. The recoil of the heavy rifle made me rock, as I stood unsteadily on my perch, and I failed to hit the brain. But the bullet, only missing the brain by an inch or two, brought the elephant to its knees; as it rose I floored it with the second barrel.[4]

Roosevelt left Africa to spend four months in Europe, where he paid courtesy calls on monarchs of different countries. Roosevelt grew weary of the formal ceremonies. Near the end of the trip he said, "If I ever meet another king, I think I shall bite him."[5]

The former President returned home in June 1910. A huge hero's welcome was waiting. There was a miniature navy of battleships, destroyers, and other boats in New York Harbor to greet him when his ship steamed in. A giant parade marched through the streets of New York in his honor. Roosevelt responded, ". . . I am more glad than I can say to get home, to be back in my own country, back among the people I love."[6]

Later that summer, Roosevelt had another adventure. He became the first former President to fly in an airplane. Airplanes at that time were open and made mostly of wood, cloth, and wire. Flying was considered risky. The flight lasted just a matter of minutes. As the plane descended, Roosevelt exclaimed in glee, "Bully! Bully! This is bully!"[7]

Back on the ground there were bigger concerns. Roosevelt had expected Taft to continue his progressive policies. On his return, Roosevelt discovered Taft's policies were more conservative than he liked. Roosevelt was so unhappy with Taft that he decided to run again for President in 1912.

There was a problem. Roosevelt had said years earlier that he would not run for a third term. He solved that dilemma by announcing that the promise applied only to three consecutive terms.[8] Although Roosevelt won most of the Republican primaries, Taft was chosen

In 1910, Theodore Roosevelt became the first former United States President to fly in an airplane.

as the party nominee. Party bosses still made most political decisions regardless of primary results.

Roosevelt chose to run on a third party ticket, the Progressive party. When he told reporters he felt as strong as a bull moose (a male moose), his party began calling itself the Bull Moose party. It adopted the bull moose as its symbol. Two major issues in Roosevelt's platform were the right of women to vote (known as "woman suffrage") and an end to child labor.

Roosevelt's physical strength helped save his life late in the campaign. On October 14, 1912, he was in Milwaukee, Wisconsin. As he stood to speak in a convertible limousine, a man in the crowd pulled a gun out of his vest and shot Roosevelt.

The gunman was an immigrant from Germany named John N. Schrank. He objected to any person running for a third term as President. He also claimed that McKinley's ghost had inspired him. Schrank was convinced that McKinley's ghost had appeared to him and told him that Roosevelt was his true murderer.

Schrank's bullet passed through the breast pocket of Roosevelt's shirt. In the pocket, Roosevelt had a metal eyeglass case and a speech folded four times over. The case and a hundred thicknesses of paper slowed the bullet's speed.

Roosevelt coughed into his hand and saw no blood. He took that as a sign that he was not seriously injured. Amazingly, he went ahead and gave a fifty-minute-long speech as planned. Only afterward did he get medical treatment.

Roosevelt spent about a week recovering from the gunshot. By the second evening, he was joking with the hospital staff. He said the night in the hospital would be the "'first real comfortable evening to himself' he had enjoyed in many days."[9]

(In a trial, Schrank was found insane and committed to a mental institution. He died there in 1943.)

Roosevelt continued campaigning, but it was a hopeless contest. He and Taft split the Republican vote. That gave Democrat Woodrow Wilson an easy victory. Wilson earned 435 electoral votes. Roosevelt finished second with 88. Taft earned only 8 electoral votes. It was the lowest total ever for a sitting President.[10]

At fifty-four years old, Roosevelt was still fairly young. So, as they had done four years earlier, Roosevelt

SOURCE DOCUMENT

I will deliver this speech or die, one or the other. . . . Friends, I shall ask you to be very quiet and please excuse me from making a very long speech. I'll do the best I can, but, you see, there is a bullet in my body. But it's nothing. I'm not hurt badly.

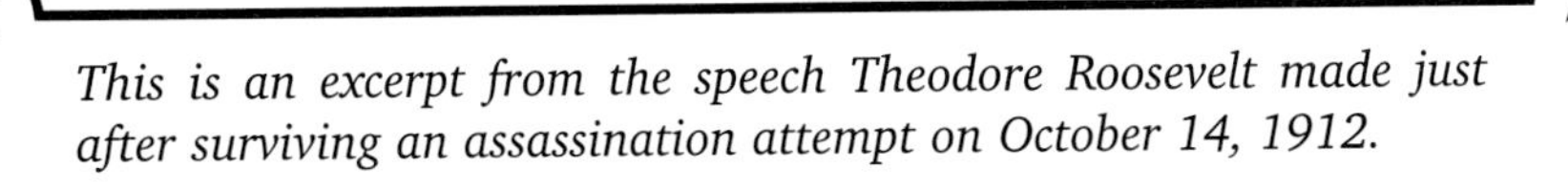

This is an excerpt from the speech Theodore Roosevelt made just after surviving an assassination attempt on October 14, 1912.

and Kermit went on an exotic journey. This time the destination was Brazil. It happened that Kermit was living in Brazil at the time. He was employed by a Brazilian railroad company. Kermit took time off from work to join his father on this new adventure.

The Roosevelts were hired to help chart an unmapped river in the jungle. It was known as the River of Doubt. The trip was sponsored by the government of Brazil and the American Museum of Natural History. Roosevelt would write about his experiences for the magazine, *Scribner's*. This trip was even more dangerous than the one to Africa. Roosevelt did not mind the risks. He said, "I have to go! It's my last chance to be a boy!"[11]

This journey was a nightmare. The jungle was loaded with insects that inflicted painful bites, even through clothing. One crew member died when his boat capsized. Another went insane and killed another member of the crew.

Roosevelt came close to dying. First he contracted malaria, a disease of the tropics. People with malaria suffer high fevers, chills, and other symptoms. Then he gashed open his leg in a canoe accident. For two days he was on the verge of death. Roosevelt was delirious, reciting lines of poetry out of the blue.

Roosevelt slowly recovered but could not walk. As the crew was about to move on, Roosevelt asked Kermit to leave him behind to die. Of course, Kermit did not leave his father, who had to be carried the rest of the way.

In spite of his agony, Roosevelt did not neglect his writing assignment. At the top of one page he scribbled, "This is not written very clearly; my temperature is 105 degrees."[12]

Two months and fifteen hundred miles later, the crew finished their task. They had successfully mapped the river. The government of Brazil renamed it Rio Roosevelt. Theodore Roosevelt emerged from the trip severely weakened. He had lost fifty-five pounds over the course of the expedition.[13]

Roosevelt's writings were turned into another book, *Through the Brazilian Wilderness.* At one point in the book, he described a typical meal: "We found and ate wild pineapples. Wild beans were in flower. At dinner we had a toucan and a couple of parrots, which were very good."[14]

Elsewhere he wrote, "This day we caught twenty-eight big fish, mostly piranhas, and everybody had all he could eat for dinner and for breakfast the following morning."[15]

In Central America one of Roosevelt's dreams was finally fulfilled. The Panama Canal was completed in 1914. Amid the celebrations, Roosevelt received some bad news. While Roosevelt was in Brazil, the Wilson administration had negotiated a treaty with the nation of Colombia. In the treaty, the United States apologized for taking the canal zone the way it did years earlier. The United States also agreed to pay Colombia $25 million in exchange for its earlier actions.

The United States Senate did not approve Wilson's treaty because many senators believed the United States had done nothing to apologize for. Still, Roosevelt took the treaty as a personal insult. For the rest of his life he hated Woodrow Wilson.[16] (After Wilson left office, a treaty with Colombia was passed. It called for the payment but no apology to Colombia.)

In the summer of 1914, World War I broke out in Europe. On one side were the countries of Serbia, Great Britain, France, and Russia. On the other side were Austria-Hungary (Austria and Hungary were one country at the time), Germany, Turkey, and Bulgaria. The basic causes of the war were years of ethnic hatred and rivalries between the peoples of southeastern Europe, known as the Balkan Peninsula.

The United States was officially neutral. However, its sympathies were with Great Britain and its allies. The opposing country with the strongest military was Germany. By early 1915, Roosevelt thought the United States should enter the war. Then in May 1915, a German submarine torpedoed an unarmed British ocean liner called the *Lusitania.* Over eleven hundred men, women, and children were killed.[17]

Anti-German sentiment swept across America. Roosevelt scolded, "This represents not merely piracy, but piracy on a vaster scale of murder than old-time pirates ever practiced . . . It is warfare against innocent men, women, and children . . ."[18]

Still, the United States stayed neutral.

In 1916, Roosevelt tried to get the Republican nomination for President. In speeches, he cried out not only against Germany, but also German Americans. The Republican old guard was offended by his comments attacking American citizens because of their ancestry. They also resented him for splitting the party in the 1912 election.

The Republican nomination went to a former New York governor named Charles Evans Hughes. The Bull Moose party then sought Roosevelt. Since Roosevelt did not think a third party could be elected, he turned them down. Roosevelt threw his support to Hughes.

Woodrow Wilson ran for a second term under the slogan, "He kept us out of war." In November, Wilson won a second term by a very narrow margin. He received 277 electoral votes to Hughes's 254.[19]

German submarines continued attacking Allied ships. These included American merchant vessels. Also, Americans learned that Germany had sent a scary message to Mexico. In it, Germany tried to convince Mexico to declare war on the United States if the United States declared war on Germany. This message became known as the Zimmermann Telegram. Just five months after Wilson was reelected, the United States officially entered the war.

Roosevelt thought it was about time. Anxious to do what he considered his fair share, he asked Wilson for permission to lead a military division overseas. After all, he had been a hero twenty years earlier in Cuba.

Roosevelt used anti-German sentiment in his speeches in 1916 in the hope of winning the Republican nomination for President.

Wilson turned down his request. He said he did not believe Roosevelt's division would ". . . contribute to the immediate success of the war."[20]

Roosevelt was disappointed and angry.[21] He complained, "I wanted to go to the war, and the people wanted me to go. I keep my good health by having a very bad temper, kept under good control."[22]

Maybe Wilson thought Roosevelt's military experience was limited. Perhaps Wilson thought Roosevelt was out of touch with modern methods of battle. Then again, it is possible that he would not do a favor for a political enemy. Wilson's true reason for rejecting Roosevelt's request is not known.

Roosevelt's granddaughter Edith Derby Williams later said of Roosevelt that the rejection "broke his heart. He wanted to go so badly. He never forgave President Wilson for that. In fact, none of us have."[23]

Roosevelt's four sons all fought. Roosevelt supported the war cause by speaking across the country. Some of his speeches seemed to cross the line from patriotism to bigotry. He again attacked some German Americans as well as conscientious objectors (persons who oppose all war because of religious or moral reasons). He seemed more like a warmonger and less like the open-minded man of earlier years.

In 1918, there was horrible news from overseas. An airplane Quentin Roosevelt was flying was shot down over Germany. It was soon confirmed that Quentin was dead. Roosevelt was filled with grief. A friend said that

Roosevelt was no longer the enthusiastic and excited man he once had been. The friend said of Roosevelt, the "boy in him had died."[24]

Historian and author David McCullough said that Roosevelt realized his ideas about the glory of war were false. McCullough noted, "All of his old romantic ideas about war as the great chance to be a man, to serve your country and to be heroic, all of that was destroyed. And he must have understood how much of what he'd felt and believed in was ultimately proven wrong."[25]

On November 11, 1918, the war ended with an Allied victory. Some of Roosevelt's admirers talked about him as a presidential candidate in 1920. Roosevelt answered, "I would not lift a finger to get the nomination. Since Quentin's death the world seems to have shut down on me . . ."[26]

On January 6, 1919, Theodore Roosevelt died in his sleep of a blood clot. He was sixty years old.

David McCullough said that Roosevelt "died of a broken heart, I think, probably as much as anything else."[27]

Roosevelt was buried in a public cemetery in Oyster Bay. It is just a short distance from Roosevelt's beloved home, Sagamore Hill.

9
LEGACY

After Theodore Roosevelt's death, Edith Roosevelt traveled widely and worked in local Republican politics. She died at age eighty-seven in 1948.

Daughter Alice lived until 1980, dying at age ninety-six. She resided in Washington, D.C., all her life, and remained as independent as she was in her youth. Alice mixed with Presidents and other dignitaries and became known for her biting humor and sharp tongue. For example, she once wrote about President Lyndon Johnson, "He used to complain that he couldn't kiss me under my hat and I told him that's why I wore it."[1]

Roosevelt's other daughter, Ethel, became a nurse and married a doctor. She lived quietly until her death in 1977.

Roosevelt's three surviving sons served in the military during World War II as well as World War I. Like his father, Theodore Roosevelt, Jr., became assistant secretary of the Navy. He held the post under Presidents Warren G. Harding and Calvin Coolidge. Later, he was appointed governor of Puerto Rico and governor-general of the Philippines. Theodore, Jr., died of natural causes in France during World War II in 1944.

Kermit became an executive with a steamship company. Kermit also died of natural causes in 1943 while on duty during World War II.

Archie carved out a career as a banker. He was severely wounded by shrapnel during World War II. Archie survived and lived until 1979.

Theodore Roosevelt's legacy outlived his children. Some Presidents are popular in their time, but are viewed by history as poor Presidents. Ulysses S. Grant and Calvin Coolidge are examples. Others are generally disliked while in office, but history has shown them to be among the best. Abraham Lincoln and Harry Truman fit in this category.

Few Presidents fit the category Theodore Roosevelt does. He was admired while in office and is still considered by historians to be one of the nation's great Presidents.

In 1982, a survey was taken of nearly 850 historians. They were asked to rank the Presidents in order of greatness. Of thirty-six Presidents, Theodore Roosevelt was ranked number five.[2]

SOURCE DOCUMENT

I am sorry to learn of his death. He was a great American. His loss will be a great one for the country.

This is the statement made by John N. Schrank, the man who attempted to assassinate Theodore Roosevelt, after hearing of the former President's death in 1919.

The same year, the *Chicago Tribune* conducted a similar but smaller survey. A total of forty-nine historians were questioned. In that survey, Theodore Roosevelt finished fourth.[3]

Most historians believe Roosevelt made the correct decisions and pushed for the right policies. They say he improved the capitalist system by breaking up unfair trusts. Thanks to Roosevelt, we are confident that meat and other foods we buy at the grocery store are safe to eat.

Our vast national park system exists due to Roosevelt's example. Roosevelt is called the father of the modern Navy. Yet, he also won the Nobel Peace Prize and the title of peacemaker.

Roosevelt championed views that were controversial in his day but are accepted today as morally right. These include woman suffrage and an end to child labor. He sided with the poor and oppressed minorities, such as coal miners, African Americans, and Jews. With his very manner Roosevelt filled the spirit of the American people with confidence.

Historian Edmund Morris summed up Roosevelt's appeal. Morris wrote, "He loved being President and was so good at his job that the American people loved him for loving it."[4]

On the other hand, Roosevelt has critics. Historian Kathleen Brady called Roosevelt the most overrated figure in American history. She wrote,

> Roosevelt was a "trustbuster" who was selective in his targets . . . He was a "conservationist" who himself slaughtered buffalo and caribou, and a heroic "Rough Rider" who could have been more effective, if less celebrated, had he retained his post as Undersecretary of the Navy . . .[5]

Others fault Roosevelt for what they consider his use of gunboat diplomacy. The example most often brought up is the Panama Canal. The executive director of the Theodore Roosevelt Association, John Gable, disagrees. Gable responds, "The Colombians were bandits. Roosevelt's critics treat them with dignity, but they had broken their word again and again and again."[6]

Some criticize Roosevelt's love of blood sports. How could a man who believed so strongly in conservation also enjoy killing animals? Roosevelt mounted hunting trophies on the walls at Sagamore Hill. One can see them there today.

Those who defend Roosevelt say he hunted honorably. They add that it is impossible to separate a person from the times in which he or she lived. A nature writer named Paul Schullery wrote, "By the standards of his day Roosevelt's attitudes were most enlightened and his bags [animals captured] were selective and modest."[7]

From Roosevelt's time through the 1970s, most United States Presidents have followed his policies of an activist government. The exceptions are Harding, Coolidge, and Herbert Hoover, who served consecutively from 1921 to 1933. One of the most vigorous followers of Roosevelt's example was his political enemy, Woodrow Wilson. During Wilson's administration, the first child labor law was passed. Also, the Nineteenth Amendment to the Constitution became law under Wilson. It gave women the right to vote.

Perhaps the most activist President since Wilson was Roosevelt's cousin, Franklin Delano Roosevelt. Known as FDR, he was elected President in 1932. Under FDR, a law was passed in 1938 banning child labor in interstate industries. It was called the Fair Labor Standards Act. The Glass-Steagall Act was passed under FDR in 1933. It made sure that the money we deposit in banks is insured. Like Theodore Roosevelt, Woodrow Wilson and Franklin Roosevelt are ranked by historians as two of the best Presidents.

Roosevelt's niece Eleanor was one of the most active First Ladies. Like her uncle, she was highly regarded for her compassion and concern for the poor and oppressed.

Since Ronald Reagan became President in 1981, the

Franklin Delano Roosevelt followed his cousin Theodore Roosevelt's example and followed activist policies when he became President. This is the only known photograph of Theodore (left) and Franklin Roosevelt (right) together.

United States presidency and Congress have moved away from an activist approach to public policy. A prevailing attitude is that government regulations hurt honest capitalism.

This seems to contradict Roosevelt's reformist views. Then why is he still ranked so highly?

Some of Roosevelt's critics say it is because Roosevelt is judged as a folk hero rather than by what he accomplished. Others say that Roosevelt's policies were right, but government has grown too big since his time. They say government should protect us from eating tainted meat but should not try to solve every problem.

Carved into a mountain called Mount Rushmore in South Dakota are the likenesses of four Presidents: George Washington, Thomas Jefferson, Abraham Lincoln, and Theodore Roosevelt. Most Americans believe Roosevelt is right at home there, as one of the country's greatest leaders.

Chronology

1858—Born in New York City on October 27.

1876–1880—Attends and graduates from Harvard University.

1880—Marries Alice Lee on October 27.

1881—Elected to New York State Assembly.

1884—Daughter Alice born on February 12; wife and mother both die on February 14; moves to Dakota Territory.

1886—Moves back to New York City; loses mayoral election; marries Edith Carow on December 2.

1887—Settles at Sagamore Hill in Oyster Bay, New York; son Theodore, Jr., is born.

1889—Begins work as civil service commissioner in Benjamin Harrison administration; son Kermit is born.

1891—Daughter Ethel is born.

1894—Son Archibald is born.

1895—Becomes New York City police commissioner.

1897—Son Quentin is born.

1898—Leads charge up San Juan Hill in Spanish-American War; elected governor of New York.

1900—Elected Vice President of the United States under William McKinley.

1901—Becomes President of the United States on September 14 after McKinley dies from assassin's bullet.

1902—Sues J.P. Morgan's Northern Securities Company; helps settle coal miners' strike.

1903—Creates Department of Commerce and Labor; obtains Panama Canal zone.

1904—Construction of Panama Canal begins; wins suit against Northern Securities Company as court makes decision; elected President in his own right; announces Roosevelt Corollary.

1905—Sends United States personnel to take over Santo Domingo customs office; mediates Russo-Japanese War; holds football reform conference.

1906—Reform policies accepted by Congress as Hepburn Act, Pure Food and Drug Act, and Meat Inspection Act are passed; visits Panama Canal construction site; awarded Nobel Peace Prize.

1907—Arranges gentlemen's agreement with Japan; Panic of 1907 occurs; Great White Fleet departs.

1908—Great White Fleet receives warm welcome in Japan.

1909—Great White Fleet returns; leaves presidency on March 4; departs for Africa.

1910—Returns from Africa to a hero's welcome.

1912—Runs for President on Progressive (Bull Moose) party and loses; survives assassination attempt.

1913—Takes trip to Brazil.

1914—Panama Canal completed.

1917—Makes request to head military division in World War I but is turned down.

1918—Quentin dies in World War I.

1919—Dies on January 6.

Chapter Notes

Chapter 1

1. Shumpei Okamoto, *The Japanese Oligarchy and the Russo-Japanese War* (New York: Columbia University Press, 1970), p. 128.

2. Clifton Daniel, editor in chief, *Chronicle of the 20th Century* (Liberty, Miss.: JL International Publishing, 1992), p. 75.

3. Peter Spry-Leverton and Peter Kornicki, *Japan* (New York: Facts on File Publications, 1988), p. 71.

4. Eugene P. Trani, *The Treaty of Portsmouth* (Lexington, Ky.: University of Kentucky Press, 1969), p. 57.

5. Ibid.

Chapter 2

1. Nathan Miller, *The Roosevelt Chronicles* (Garden City, N.Y.: Doubleday & Company, Inc., 1979), p. 4.

2. Theodore Roosevelt, *An Autobiography* (New York: Da Capo Press, Inc., 1913, 1925), p. 5.

3. Ibid.

4. Ibid., p. 13.

5. Corinne Roosevelt Robinson, *My Brother Theodore Roosevelt* (New York: Charles Scribner's Sons, 1921), p. 23.

6. David McCullough, *Mornings on Horseback* (New York: Simon and Schuster, 1981), p. 57.

7. Personal interview with John Gable, Executive Director, Theodore Roosevelt Association, February 25, 1996.

8. McCullough, p. 58.

9. Roosevelt, p. 14.

10. McCullough, p. 28.

11. Roosevelt, p. 7.

12. Ibid., p. 13.

13. Nathan Miller, *Theodore Roosevelt: A Life* (New York: William Morrow and Company, Inc., 1992), p. 42.

14. Henry F. Pringle, *Theodore Roosevelt* (New York: Smithmark Publishers, Inc., 1931, 1995), p. 29.

15. Robinson, p. 50.

16. Roosevelt, p. 18.

17. Edmund Morris, *The Rise of Theodore Roosevelt* (New York: Coward, McCann & Geoghegan, Inc., 1979) p. 63.

18. Miller, *Theodore Roosevelt: A Life,* p. 55.

Chapter 3

1. Paul F. Boller, Jr., *Presidential Anecdotes* (New York: Oxford University Press, 1981), p. 201.

2. Edmund Morris, *The Rise of Theodore Roosevelt* (New York: Coward, McCann & Geoghegan, Inc., 1979), p. 97.

3. Nathan Miller, *The Roosevelt Chronicles* (Garden City, N.Y.: Doubleday & Company, Inc., 1979), p. 186.

4. Edmund Morris, "Theodore Roosevelt, President," *American Heritage,* June/July 1981, p. 8.

5. David McCullough, *Mornings on Horseback* (New York: Simon and Schuster, 1981), p. 223.

6. Nathan Miller, *Theodore Roosevelt: A Life* (New York: William Morrow and Company, Inc., 1992), p. 97.

7. McCullough, p. 224.

8. Miller, *Theodore Roosevelt: A Life,* p. 100.

9. Miller, *The Roosevelt Chronicles,* p. 188.

10. Miller, *Theodore Roosevelt: A Life,* p. 103.

11. Ibid., p. 127.

12. William Henry Harbaugh, *Power and Responsibility: The Life and Times of Theodore Roosevelt* (New York: Collier Books, 1963), p. 40.

13. United Press International, "Roosevelt Courtship Letters Speak Softly," *Keene Sentinel,* June 6, 1986, p. 14.

14. McCullough, p. 283.

15. Miller, *Theodore Roosevelt: A Life,* p. 155.

16. David C. Whitney, *The American Presidents* (Garden City, N.Y.: Doubleday & Company, 1978), p. 218.

17. Miller, *Theodore Roosevelt: A Life,* p. 158.

18. *The American Experience,* "TR: The Story of Theodore Roosevelt," WGBH Educational Foundation and David Grubin Productions, Inc., 1996.

Chapter 4

1. Theodore Roosevelt, *An Autobiography* (New York: Da Capo Press, Inc., 1913, 1925), p. 122.

2. Ibid.

3. Maltese Cross Cabin handout, National Park Service, Theodore Roosevelt National Park.

4. Mario R. DiNunzio, ed., *Theodore Roosevelt, An American Mind: Selected Writings* (New York: Penguin Books, 1995), p. 281.

5. Edmund Morris, *The Rise of Theodore Roosevelt* (New York: Coward, McCann & Geoghegan, Inc., 1979), p. 357.

6. Personal interview with John Gable, Executive Director, Theodore Roosevelt Association, March 22, 1996.

7. Hermann Hagedorn and Gary G. Roth, *Sagamore Hill: An Historic Guide* (Oyster Bay, N.Y.: Theodore Roosevelt Association, 1977), p. 12.

8. David McCullough, *Mornings on Horseback* (New York: Simon and Schuster, 1981), p. 359.

9. Personal interview with Amy Verone, Curator, Sagamore Hill National Historic Site, September 16, 1996.

10. Nathan Miller, *The Roosevelt Chronicles* (Garden City, N.Y.: Doubleday & Company, Inc., 1979), p. 236.

11. Ibid.

12. *The Indomitable Teddy Roosevelt,* directed and produced by Harrison Engle, Gannett Co., Inc., 1983.

13. Michael Teague, *Mrs. L.: Conversations with Alice Roosevelt Longworth* (Garden City, N.Y.: Doubleday & Company, Inc., 1981), p. 110.

14. Personal interview with John Gable, Executive Director, Theodore Roosevelt Association, March 22, 1996.

15. Henry F. Pringle, *Theodore Roosevelt* (New York: Smithmark Publishers, Inc., 1931, 1995), p. 123.

16. Ibid., p. 124.

17. *A Walk Through the Twentieth Century,* "TR and His Times" episode, created and developed by The Corporation for Entertainment and Learning, Inc., and Bill Moyers, CEL/BDM, 1983.

18. *The Indomitable Teddy Roosevelt.*

19. Samuel Fallows, ed., *Life of William McKinley: Our Martyred President* (Chicago: Regan Printing House, 1901), p. 352.

20. *Biography,* "Theodore Roosevelt: Rough Rider to Rushmore" episode, produced by Greystone Productions, Inc., for A&E Network, 1995.

21. Ibid.

22. Roosevelt, p. 259.

23. *The Indomitable Teddy Roosevelt.*

24. Arthur S. Link, "The President As Progressive," in *Every Four Years,* ed. Robert C. Post, (New York: W. W. Norton & Company, 1980), p. 154.

Chapter 5

1. Theodore Roosevelt, *An Autobiography* (New York: Da Capo Press, Inc., 1913, 1925), p. 349.

2. Personal interview with Mark Comito, Interpreter, Theodore Roosevelt Inaugural National Historic Site, March 22, 1996.

3. Ibid.

4. Edmund Morris, "Theodore Roosevelt, President," *American Heritage,* June/July 1981, p. 5.

5. Paul F. Boller, Jr., *Presidential Anecdotes* (New York: Oxford University Press, 1981), p. 198.

6. *A Walk Through the Twentieth Century,* "TR and His Times" episode, created and developed by The Corporation for Entertainment and Learning, Inc., and Bill Moyers, CEL/BDM, 1983.

7. *The Indomitable Teddy Roosevelt,* directed and produced by Harrison Engle, Gannett Co., Inc., 1983.

8. Nathan Miller, *Theodore Roosevelt: A Life* (New York: William Morrow and Company, Inc., 1992), p. 368.

9. Clifton Daniel, editor in chief, *Chronicle of the 20th Century* (Liberty, Miss.: JL International Publishing, 1992), p. 40.

10. Henry F. Pringle, *Theodore Roosevelt* (New York: Smithmark Publishers, Inc., 1931, 1995), p. 190.

11. William Henry Harbaugh, *Power and Responsibility: The Life and Times of Theodore Roosevelt* (New York: Collier Books, 1963), p. 178.

12. Personal interview with John Gable, Executive Director, Theodore Roosevelt Association, April 12, 1996.

13. William Davison Johnston, *TR: Champion of the Strenuous Life* (New York: Theodore Roosevelt Association, 1958, 1984), p. 54.

14. Paul F. Boller, Jr., *Presidential Anecdotes* (New York: Oxford University Press, 1981), p. 207.

15. Johnston, p. 92.

16. Ibid., and Harbaugh, p. 315.

17. Paul Schullery, ed., *Theodore Roosevelt, Wilderness Writings: Literature of the American Wilderness* (Salt Lake City: Peregrine Smith Books, 1986), p. 217.

Chapter 6

1. David C. Whitney, *The American Presidents* (Garden City, N.Y.: Doubleday & Company, 1978), p. 221.

2. Theodore Roosevelt, *An Autobiography* (New York: Da Capo Press, Inc., 1913, 1925), pp. 524-527.

3. Ibid., pp. 514-516.

4. Personal interview with John Gable, Executive Director, Theodore Roosevelt Association, March 22, 1996.

5. *The Indomitable Teddy Roosevelt,* directed and produced by Harrison Engle, Gannet Co., Inc., 1983.

6. Paul F. Boller, Jr., *Presidential Campaigns* (New York: Oxford University Press, 1985), p. 183.

7. Hermann Hagedorn, *The Roosevelt Family of Sagamore Hill* (New York: The Macmillan Company, 1954), p. 253.

8. Ibid., pp. 146-147.

9. Lonnelle Aikman, *The Living White House* (Washington, D.C.: White House Historical Association and National Geographic Society, 1982), p. 84.

10. Paul F. Boller, Jr., *Presidential Wives* (New York: Oxford University Press, 1988), p. 199.

11. Michael Teague, *Mrs. L.: Conversations with Alice Roosevelt Longworth* (Garden City, N.Y.: Doubleday & Company, Inc., 1981), p. 82.

12. Aikman, p. 84.

13. Paul F. Boller, Jr., *Presidential Anecdotes* (New York: Oxford University Press, 1981), p. 206.

14. *The American Experience,* "TR: The Story of Theodore Roosevelt," WGBH Educational Foundation and David Grubin Productions, Inc., 1996.

15. Ibid.

16. Roosevelt, *An Autobiography,* p. 387.

17. Clifton Daniel, editor in chief, *Chronicle of the 20th Century* (Liberty, Miss.: JL International Publishing, 1992), p. 72.

18. Geoffrey Ward, *Before the Trumpet: Young Franklin Roosevelt 1882-1905* (New York: Harper & Row Publishers, 1985), p. 340.

19. John S. Watterson, "Inventing Modern Football," *American Heritage,* September/October 1988, p. 106.

20. Ibid., p. 113.

21. *The Indomitable Teddy Roosevelt.*

22. Upton Sinclair, *The Jungle* (Cambridge, Mass.: Robert Bentley, Inc., 1905, 1946), p. vi.

23. William Henry Harbaugh, *Power and Responsibility: The Life and Times of Theodore Roosevelt* (New York: Collier Books, 1963), pp. 256-257.

24. John Spargo, *The Bitter Cry of the Children* (Chicago: Quadrangle Books, 1906, 1968), p. 164.

25. Ibid., p. 153.

26. *The Indomitable Teddy Roosevelt.*

27. Daniel, p. 95.

Chapter 7

1. Henry F. Pringle, *Theodore Roosevelt* (New York: Smithmark Publishers, Inc., 1931, 1995), p. 286.

2. Frederick W. Marks, III, *Velvet on Iron: The Diplomacy of Theodore Roosevelt* (Lincoln, Neb.: University of Nebraska Press, 1979), p. 56.

3. Nathan Miller, *The Roosevelt Chronicles* (Garden City, N.Y.: Doubleday & Company, Inc., 1992), p. 384.

5. Clifton Daniel, editor in chief, *Chronicle of the 20th Century* (Liberty, Miss.: JL International Publishing, 1992), p. 107.

6. Paul F. Boller, Jr., *Presidential Campaigns* (New York: Oxford University Press, 1985), p. 189.

7. Daniel, p. 112.

8. Boller, *Presidential Campaigns,* p. 189.

9. Ibid.

10. Theodore Roosevelt, *An Autobiography* (New York: Da Capo Press, Inc., 1913, 1925), p. 548.

Chapter 8

1. Henry F. Pringle, *Theodore Roosevelt* (New York: Smithmark Publishers, Inc., 1931, 995), p. 358.

2. William Davison Johnston, *TR: Champion of the Strenuous Life* (New York: Theodore Roosevelt Association, 1958, 1984), p. 99.

3. Mario R. DiNunzio, ed., *Theodore Roosevelt, An American Mind: Selected Writings* (New York: Penguin Books, 1995), p. 223.

4. Ibid., p. 219.

5. *The Indomitable Teddy Roosevelt,* directed and produced by Harrison Engle, Gannet Co., Inc., 1983.

6. Johnston, p. 106.

7. *The Indomitable Teddy Roosevelt.*

8. Paul F. Boller, Jr., *Presidential Campaigns* (New York: Oxford University Press, 1985), p. 192.

9. *The Boston Herald,* "Doctors Tell T.R. That Quiet is Chief Need," October 16, 1912, p. 1.

10. David C. Whitney, *The American Presidents* (Garden City, N.Y.: Doubleday & Company, 1978), p. 401.

11. Nathan Miller, *The Roosevelt Chronicles* (Garden City, N.Y.: Doubleday & Company, Inc., 1979), p. 284.

12. Edmund Morris, "As a literary lion, Roosevelt preached what he practiced," *Smithsonian,* November 1983, p. 86.

13. *Biography,* "Theodore Roosevelt: Rough Rider to Rushmore" episode, produced by Greystone Productions, Inc., for A&E Network, 1995.

14. DiNunzio, p. 229.

15. Ibid., p. 236.

16. Pringle, pp. 406-407.

17. Allan Nevins and Henry Steele Commager, *A Pocket History of the United States* (New York: Pocket Books, 1981), p. 394.

18. William Henry Harbaugh, *Power and Responsibility: The Life and Times of Theodore Roosevelt* (New York: Collier Books, 1963), p. 448.

19. Boller, *Presidential Campaigns,* p. 206.

20. Harbaugh, p. 472.

21. Hermann Hagedorn, *The Roosevelt Family of Sagamore Hill* (New York: The Macmillan Company, 1954), p. 365.

22. Ibid.

23. *The American Experience,* "TR: The Story of Theodore Roosevelt," WGBH Educational Foundation and David Grubin Productions, Inc., 1996.

24. Nathan Miller, *The Roosevelt Chronicles,* p. 289.

25. *The American Experience,* "TR: The Story of Theodore Roosevelt."

26. William Manners, *TR and Will* (New York: Harcourt, Brace & World, Inc., 1969), p. 308.

27. *A Walk Through the Twentieth Century,* "TR and His Times" episode, created and developed by the Corporation for Entertainment and Learning, Inc., and Bill Moyers, CEL/BDM, 1983.

Chapter 9

1. Michael Teague, *Mrs. L.: Conversations with Alice Roosevelt Longworth* (Garden City, N.Y.: Doubleday & Company, Inc., 1981), p. 199.

2. Robert K. Murray and Tim H. Blessing, "The Presidential Performance Study: A Progress Report," *The Journal of American History,* December 1983, p. 540.

3. Ibid.

4. Edmund Morris, "Theodore Roosevelt, President," *American Heritage,* June/July 1981, p. 15.

5. *American Heritage,* "Overrated & Underrated Americans," July/August 1988, p. 50.

6. Personal interview with John Gable, Executive Director, Theodore Roosevelt Association, April 12, 1996.

7. Paul Schullery, ed., *Theodore Roosevelt, Wilderness Writings: Literature of the American Wilderness* (Salt Lake City: Peregrine Smith Books, 1986), p. 20.

Places to Visit

Connecticut

Museum of American Political Life, West Hartford.
The history of every presidential campaign in the United States is told through buttons, banners, photos, and videotape. Open year round. (860) 768-4090.

Georgia

Bulloch Hall, Roswell (outside Atlanta).
This is the girlhood home of Theodore Roosevelt's mother, Mittie Bulloch Roosevelt. Open weekdays year round. (770) 992-1731.

Indiana

College Football Hall of Fame, South Bend.
A multimedia look at the sport's heritage and history, including Roosevelt's help in founding the NCAA. Open weekdays, year round. (219) 235-9999.

New York

Theodore Roosevelt Birthplace National Historic Site, New York City.
The President's birthplace has been reconstructed to look as it did when he was growing up. The adjacent house contains a museum devoted to Roosevelt's life. Open Wednesday through Sunday, year round. (212) 260-1616.

Sagamore Hill National Historic Site, Oyster Bay.
Visitors can explore Roosevelt's adult home which looks as it

did when Roosevelt was President. Within walking distance is the Old Orchard Museum, with exhibits on Roosevelt's life. Open year round. (516) 922-4447.

Theodore Roosevelt Inaugural National Historic Site, Buffalo. This is the mansion where Roosevelt was sworn in as President following William McKinley's assassination. Exhibits pertaining to the assassination and inauguration are on view. Open year round. (716) 884-0095.

North Dakota

Theodore Roosevelt National Park, near Medora.
A large portion of the rugged badlands where Roosevelt lived and worked is preserved. Roosevelt's original Maltese Cross cabin is in the park. Open year round. (701) 623-4466.

South Dakota

Mount Rushmore National Memorial, near Keystone.
Roosevelt is one of the four Presidents memorialized in this famous mountain sculpture. Open year round.
(605) 574-2523.

Washington, D.C.

Theodore Roosevelt Island.
A granite sculpture of Roosevelt is the centerpiece of this wilderness preserve in the Potomac River. Four granite tablets are inscribed with Roosevelt quotes. Open year round. (703) 285-2598.

The White House.
Several rooms are open to visitors on certain weekday mornings. You can get tickets when you arrive or in advance through your senator or congressperson. Open year round. (202) 456-7041.

Internet Addresses

The National Park Service ParkNet includes: Theodore Roosevelt Birthplace National Historic Site, Sagamore Hill National Historic Site, Theodore Roosevelt Inaugural National Historic Site, Theodore Roosevelt National Park, Mount Rushmore National Memorial, and Theodore Roosevelt Island.

The National Park Service

home page — http://www.nps.gov

Theodore Roosevelt Association

E-mail — tra@sprynet.com

White House Historical Association

E-mail — whh@erols.com

College Football Hall of Fame

home page — http://collegefootball.org/

Further Reading

Freedman, Russell. *Kids at Work: Lewis Hine and the Crusade Against Child Labor.* New York: Clarion Books, 1994.

Kent, Zachary. *The Story of the Rough Riders.* Chicago: Children's Press, 1991.

———. *World War I: "The War to End Wars."* Springfield, N.J.: Enslow Publishers, 1994.

Marrin, Albert. *The Spanish-American War.* New York: Atheneum Books for Young Readers, 1991.

Meltzer, Milton. *Cheap Raw Material.* New York: Viking Press, 1994.

Roosevelt, Theodore. *A Bully Father: Theodore Roosevelt's Letters to His Children,* ed. Joan Paterson Kerr and Robert D. Loomis. New York: Random House, 1995.

———. *An Autobiography.* New York: Da Capo Press, 1913, 1941, 1985.

St. George, Judith. *Panama Canal: Gateway to the World.* New York: G. Putnam's Sons, 1989.

Sandler, Martin W. *Cowboys.* New York: HarperCollins, 1994.

Savage, Jeff. *Cowboys and Cow Towns of the Wild West.* Springfield, N.J.: Enslow Publishers, 1995.

Schwartz, Alvin. *When I Grew Up Long Ago.* New York: J.B. Lippincott Co., 1978.

Smith, Carter, ed. *The Legendary Wild West.* Brookfield, Conn.: The Millbrook Press, 1992.

Index